Discovering Clapham

Peter Jefferson Smith and Alyson Wilson

THE CLAPHAM SOCIETY

2007

Published by The Clapham Society
22 Crescent Grove, London SW4 7AH

www.outlines.org.uk/claphamsociety/

Printed by Cantate

ISBN 978 0 9500694 7 0

To the Curious Reader

Samuel Pepys, the great diarist, was once described as *'a most curious person'*. The friend who called him that meant that he was always eager to find out new things. He visited Clapham many times, and died here in 1703. **Discovering Clapham** is for curious persons, who want to know more about the place where they live. It describes where Pepys lived and died, and much else.

History can be read in books; for faraway places or vanished civilisations, that may be the main way of recalling them. But the history of near at hand, of the place where you have come to live, can also be discovered by going around and looking.

The introduction is an overview of the history of Clapham, how it developed from a little rural village to the bustling part of inner London it is today. Then each of the seven chapters takes an area of Clapham, and illustrates a selection of the interesting buildings. The captions to the pictures locate them, but you may also find a street map helpful.

Many of the historic pictures come from Lambeth Landmark, the on-line collection from Lambeth Archives (www.lambethlandmark.com), and those who want to see more of how Clapham looked in the past will find it a treasure trove. Older pictures are dated, and all the undated pictures were taken in 2005 or 2006.

Clapham changes fast. **Discovering Clapham** is a snapshot taken at the end of 2006. From it you can learn how it is, and how it came to be as it is, at the time the book was written. New years will bring new perspectives, new discoveries, new knowledge. That is what makes history alive and exciting.

Acknowledgements

The authors are grateful to many people for help with this book. The members of the Clapham Society Local History Sub-Committee have given advice and support throughout the project. In particular, Annabel Allott and Mary Coales have read and suggested improvements to the text, and Michael Green has kindly allowed us access to his research on medieval Clapham and on William Hewer's Great House, which will be used in his forthcoming book, *Historic Clapham*. Additional historical information has been kindly supplied by I S Maxwell and Chris Morley, and Michael Wilson has helped with the arduous task of proof-reading and index-checking.

Derrick McRobert has again been unfailingly long-suffering with our design requests, and Margaret Battley and her colleagues at Cantate have handled the production of the book with their customary expertise.

We are grateful to the following for help with finding illustrations and for permission to reproduce them. Unless otherwise stated, new photography is by Peter Jefferson Smith, and other uncredited illustrations are the property of the Clapham Society.

Roger Armstrong   44 (right)
Bernard Battley   8, 14, 17, 61 (top)
Janet Blencowe   31 (top)
Blossom and Browne   21
Lionel Carley   35 (left)
Captain Cook Society   42 (top)
Colin Doeg   32
The Clothworkers' Company   33
Michael Green   22 (right), 64
Trustees of Hibberts' Almshouses   18
Holy Trinity Church   28 (left), 96
Anna Jefferson Smith   75, 78, 84 (both)
Peter Jefferson Smith   6, 10, 28 (right)
Sinclair Johnston   54 (left), 71 (right)
Lambeth Archives   11, 15, 38 (bottom), 57 (top), 59, 62 (top), 67 (bottom), 68, 73
London Metropolitan Archives   46, 90
London Transport Museum   41, 63
Museum of London ©   9
National Portrait Gallery, London   22 (left), 38 (top), 94 (left)
Tim Slorick   93
Wandsworth Museum   79, 81

Discovering Clapham

Contents

Introduction – A History of Clapham

The visible history of Clapham starts in the late seventeenth century. The sixteenth and seventeenth centuries were a time of social and religious upheaval and a great cultural burgeoning. The landscape of our towns and villages changed through what one historian has called *'the great rebuilding'* of England. During the turmoil of the Reformation, the Civil War and the Glorious Revolution, an old Surrey village started to take on a shape we can recognise today.

But an older settlement lies beneath our feet. Prehistoric people left their crude implements on the Common and modern aerial photos show traces of their agriculture. **The Romans** made Stane Street, a great military road from London to Chichester. If any part survives here, it may lie under the High Street and South Side. Roman artefacts have been found, though no sign of major occupation. Some older historians tried to improve on history; but Julius Caesar did not march across the Common, nor did two third century contenders for the Empire do battle there. We reach firmer ground **in the Saxon period**, when an estate containing a small village settlement was called **Clopeham**, meaning either village on a hill or village in scrubland. That is the origin of the name: there is no connection with one Osgood Clapha, who had an estate at Lambeth where King Harthacanute died dramatically in 1042.

When William the Conqueror's officials compiled his **Domesday Book** in 1086, Clapham was one of many manors held by Geoffrey de Mandeville, one of William's wealthiest nobles. It was small; the officials noted a few villagers, plough-lands and meadow. There is no mention of a church or a mill; it does not follow that they did not exist, but if they did they were not valuable enough to be worth noting.

The history of the medieval manor and village has been obscure, but is now being pieced together, using legal records, evidence of place names and archaeology. The most fertile land lay to the north of the Common, where the ground sloped down towards the Battersea marshes and the river, and many little streams brought water from the Common. On the other sides of the Common the land was poorer and difficult to work, while the Common itself, larger than it is now, was boggy and useful only for grazing and supplying brushwood for the villagers. The village was in the Rectory Grove area, and by the early thirteenth century, if not earlier, there was a church where St Paul's now stands. There was a small moated manor house next to it. East and west of the village were the farm lands.

As in most of western Europe **in the early Middle Ages**, there was a rapid growth of population which peaked in about 1300 – even poor land on the northern edge of the Common came under the plough. But in the fourteenth century famines caused by

Clapham in 1878. From a Kelly's Post Office Directory map

Clapham Common. Lithograph by T M Baynes, 1823

disastrous weather, followed by the Black Death, caused the population to collapse. Much of the farmed area north of the Common was abandoned, to become a wooded hunting ground. We inherit from this period little more than some place names and the shape of the parish, running from the old village centre east and south to meet the boundaries of Lambeth and Streatham at the top of Lyham Road, then westwards to include Clapham Park and land round Nightingale Lane.

Early modern Clapham was shaped by incoming wealth. The medieval manor had passed through many owners of little note, until in 1583 it was bought by Bartholomew Clerke, lawyer, courtier and diplomat. He rebuilt the house in style – a big Elizabethan house with a conspicuous corner turret, and grand enough to entertain the Queen. Henry Atkins, physician to James I, bought the Manor in 1616, and it remained in his family and the related family of the Bowyers ever since.

Clerke and the Atkins family were followed by others whose wealth came from commerce. Most notable among them was the Gauden family, suppliers to the Navy under Cromwell and Charles II. Their estate included a hunting lodge, in the woods to the north of the Common. **In the early 1660s**, Sir Denis Gauden enlarged this into a great house with finely laid out gardens; and when he ran into financial problems, it was bought by William Hewer, former clerk and then business partner of Samuel Pepys. Hewer lived there in style, with a fine collection of oriental objets d'art. Another City family, the Daniels, had a mansion on land now occupied by Grafton Square.

None of these great houses have survived; old fashioned and unwanted, in a place where building land was in demand, all were replaced by later developers. But **from the end of the seventeenth** and beginning of the eighteenth centuries we have the first surviving buildings, in Old Town and along North Side by Holy Trinity Church. The parish records have started to tell us about life in Clapham. There were some merchants and tradesmen, but most people either worked on the land or served the rich. As well as the Parish Church there was a Baptist chapel, and after the restoration of Charles II the non-conformists excluded from the Church of England set up their own chapel. From at least 1648 there was a village school. Near enough to London to share its prosperity, the village also shared some of its troubles. Plague was endemic, and an outbreak in 1603 carried off the Rector (the priest in charge of the parish church) and his whole household.

Later in the century, disputes between Clapham and Battersea over which parish included the western half of the Common led to scuffles, and, happily for us, lawsuits in which the witnesses told what the Common was like. It was still mostly rough ground, valuable for free grazing for the parishioners' livestock. Exposed and windy, there was a windmill which gave

its name to the pub. The Common was also starting to be used as the place of recreation it is today; there were archery and cricket, and the gentry of Clapham laid out a long horse-racing track, starting near the windmill and going right over to the west side. Also on the Common was a spring well, which provided plentiful water to the inhabitants.

George Hibbert MP.
Painting by Sir Thomas Lawrence,
1811-12

Eighteenth century incomers were City merchants, many of them bankers. They included Henry Hoare, who laid out the gardens of his country estate at Stourhead in Wiltshire, but also wanted a country villa nearer London, and the Barclay family, bankers and brewers. The family to have the greatest impact on our history was the Thorntons; merchants from Hull trading with the Baltic, they moved to London and in 1735 bought an estate on South Side. John Thornton, born in 1720, with his friend the Revd. Henry Venn, were the first of the group known as the Clapham Sect.

Eighteenth century Clapham was changing fast. While the Common could be a dangerous place, where travellers risked robbery by footpads and highway-men, it was becoming more and more the centre of Clapham, as it was surrounded by the villas of the rich. One of them, Henton Brown, raised the mount in the Mount Pond and built a private summer-house. A banker, his clients included Benjamin Franklin, who conducted a scientific experiment on the pond. The Lords of the Manor permitted gravel digging for road building, creating large numbers of ponds. Other people tried to nibble away at common land, but the leading inhabitants generally stuck together to protect the Common as open land. One of them, an influential West Indiaman, George Hibbert, planted rare trees opposite his house on North Side. Christopher Baldwin, whose wealth also came from plantations in the West Indies, promoted a scheme to drain and level the Common and plant trees.

When Daniel Lysons described the village in 1792 he was able to say that the Common, previously *'little better than a morass'* now had the appearance of a park. He also wrote that the population appeared to have increased more rapidly than that of any other of the parishes round London which he had studied. With about 2,500 inhabitants in Lysons' time, it was to grow faster still.

One consequence of the shifting focus of the village towards the Common and the growth of population was that the old Parish Church by the Manor House, as well as being ramshackle and crowded with monuments, was too small and inconvenient. John Thornton and other leading residents carried through a scheme to build a much larger modern church, on a site on the north-east corner of the Common. Holy Trinity opened in 1776, and became the focus for the Clapham Sect.

The Clapham Sect is the name history has given to a group of friends who had been touched by the religious revival of the eighteenth century which we associate with Methodism, though unlike the Methodists they remained firmly in

the Church of England. They devoted themselves to religious and philanthropic causes. John Thornton, who when he died was said to be the second richest merchant in Europe, poured in his money, as did his son Henry. Henry brought to Clapham his relation William Wilberforce, and they formed the nucleus of the Clapham group who campaigned for the abolition of the slave trade, which Wilberforce achieved in 1807. Others in the group included Zachary Macaulay, father of the historian, who briefly ran a school in Clapham for boys from Sierra Leone.

The Thorntons secured the appointment of John Venn as Rector of Holy

Holy Trinity Church, Clapham Common, around 1790. Engraving by an unknown artist.

Trinity. He packed the Church with his preaching and led the way in providing health care and hygiene for the poor of the parish. Other Clapham Sect causes included missions abroad, bible translation and education. More contentiously, they were very conservative in politics, and campaigned for the *'reformation of manners'*, which their critics saw as taking from the poor the few pleasures they had. They had a lasting influence on the politics and morality of Victorian Britain.

In 1801 the population of the parish was 5,082: by 1901 it was 54,325. In 1801 Clapham people got to London on foot, unless they were well enough off to go on horseback or by coach. By 1901, they could go by the Tube or tram, horse-drawn but soon to be electrified, and the motor car was just starting to make an appearance. Much of this expansion was the result of the new railways, and the lie of the land made it convenient for the most important lines to skirt round Clapham. But when the London and South-Western Railway built a station on Wandsworth Common, they chose to name it Clapham Common, and in 1863, Clapham lent its name to the Junction which became the centre of neighbouring Battersea.

No previous generation had seen such a revolution, and it transformed the quiet pleasant Surrey village into a bustling suburb of a great metropolis. Writing in the 1890s, the historian Walter Besant, who had been to school at Stockwell, lamented the change:

'It is difficult, now that the whole country south of London has been covered with villas, roads, streets, and shops, to understand how wonderful for loveliness it was until the builder seized upon it. When the ground rose ... it opened out into one wild heath after another .... between the heaths stretched gardens and orchards; between the orchards were pasture lands; on the hill sides were hanging woods; .... the loveliness of South London lay at the very doors of London ... Camberwell, Brixton, Stockwell, Clapham and Wandsworth ... were separate suburbs lying each among its own gardens; the inhabitants were not clerks, but principals and employers,

North-east corner of Clapham Common with The Pavement on the left, the High Street in the centre and South Side on the right. The Alexandra (extreme right) is shown before the addition of the dome, 1866

substantial merchants and flourishing shopkeepers. [Then came the railways.] *Then the builder began; he saw that a new class of residents would be attracted by small houses and low rents. The houses sprang up as in a single night; streets in a month, churches and chapels in a quarter.'*

Up to the 1870s the builders in Clapham still aimed for people of substance. Crescent Grove (1825-27) and Grafton Square (1846-51 onwards), were enclaves of urban London planted in the Surrey village. On a much grander scale, in 1825 the great developer Thomas Cubitt acquired Bleak Hall Farm, and there started to build Clapham Park, with big villas standing detached in their own grounds. Other builders provided the smaller houses for the local tradesmen, workers and servants. Schools, churches and chapels followed; the Roman Catholics returned for the first time since the Reformation and built a fine new church in the correct medieval style. The most dominant of these new buildings were the Cedars Terraces in 1860, the work of the architect and literary man J T Knowles. The 1860s and 70s saw the building of big terraced or semi-detached houses, filling most of the remaining open lands between Old Town and Stockwell.

Clapham was noted for its seriousness and respectability: *'the man on the Clapham omnibus'* was a solid upright citizen, typifying for judges *'the reasonable man'*. For novelists like Thackeray, Clapham stood for smugness and hypocrisy, and even a friendly writer, John Thornton's grandson, wrote of a church congregation

A painted advertisement for the Music Roll Exchange, on the wall of No. 29 Clapham High Street. Painted over in 2006

of the wealthy, clad in sober-coloured, rustling silks and heavy double-milled superfine broadcloth. But it was still a place not just for wealth, but also for eminent people of worth, including the architect Sir Charles Barry, the palaeontologist Gideon Mantell and the electrical scientist J P Gassiot.

All this started to change in the 1870s, and to change very fast. The builders moved in with a new style of development; the big houses of the eighteenth century were demolished and on their gardens were laid out new streets, densely built up with standard terraced houses. Clapham was now thoroughly caught up into London, and the families who had given it such weight, financial always and moral often, had moved out to rural Surrey or over the river to Kensington. Battersea Rise, the home of Henry Thornton where Wilberforce and his friends had planned their campaigns, fell to the developer in 1907. More churches, chapels, shops, workshops and factories filled all the available spaces. Many Clapham residents commuted cheaply to the City or West End to work; but there was also a great range of local jobs. Nearby in Battersea the tangled railway network had locomotive and goods yards, and there was a tram garage in Clapham High Street. Factories and workshops made products ranging from church organs, pianos and picture frames to bicycles and motor cars. There were brewers, bakers, laundries, printers, a local newspaper, and shops in the High Street selling all you could want.

The whole environment had become urban. In the middle of the nineteenth century the Common had been maintained as an open space by a group of residents, who had filled in many of the ponds. In 1877 it was bought by the Metropolitan Board of Works as part of a policy of saving London's green spaces from the threat of development. The Board improved the planting, and its successor the London County Council built a bandstand which they treated as a focal point. There was an avenue for horse riding, there were donkey rides and boating on the ponds. A speakers' corner attracted politicians, preachers and cranks.

The later nineteenth century saw the foundation of what we now see as the normal role of the state. From 1856 power passed from the parish to the Wandsworth District Board, which became a Borough Council in 1901. The schools, formerly mostly provided by religious philanthropy, became a responsibility of the state, and the School Board for London built the schools which tower over the terraced streets like the beacons

they were seen as. A public library was built. Two pioneering women doctors founded hospitals, Annie McCall founding a maternity hospital in 1889, and, just before the First World War Maud Chadburn launching the South London Hospital for Women, opened in 1916.

Clapham was still well off and respectable; the High Street had good shops, a theatre and one of the earliest cinemas, and music thrived. The churches and chapels were still full, though not with the poorer people; Guinness Rogers, the Minister at the Congregational Church in Grafton Square, was a famed preacher and a friend of Gladstone. When Charles Booth's researchers compiled a map showing the distribution of wealth and poverty around 1900, most of the streets of Clapham were for the rich or comfortably off; one of the very few areas of real poverty was around White's Square. But, in the social scale of which the Victorians were so conscious, Clapham could be seen as a little vulgar. When Whistler wanted to vent his usual rudeness against his fellow artist and enemy Wyke Bayliss he sneered that '*I feel the folly of kicking against the parish pricks. These things are right in Clapham, by the Common*'.

Whatever the aesthetes may have thought, it is tempting for us to see early twentieth century Clapham in the golden light of an Edwardian sunset. **The First World War** shattered that; there were guns on the Common, much of which was given over to allotments and the digging of practice trenches, and the first air raids were experienced.

Young men went to the trenches, many never to return, and those that did found a changed society. Clapham was now on the border between the inner city, a land of poverty and slum clearance, and the semi-detached houses of suburbia. The builders were destroying the detached villas and gardens of the nineteenth century; Clapham Park had suburban development similar to neighbouring Streatham, while in northern Clapham there was the new phenomenon of estates of flats. Most were the austere work of the London County Council, but there were some stylish private blocks. Hightrees House, a landmark at the southern end of the Common, was completed in 1937.

Clapham was no longer a '*good address*', but still had many interesting residents. John Burns and Arthur Henderson had both come from working class origins to the Cabinet. Graham Greene set a novel in Clapham, and Dylan Thomas pursued an affair with another novelist, Pamela Hansford Johnson. But far more typical of Clapham residents between the wars was the Gibbons family, the fictitious subjects of Noel Coward's 1939 play, filmed in 1944, *This Happy Breed*. Much of it filmed in Alderbrook Road, it shows the lives of a lower middle-class family from 1919 to the outbreak of the Second World War in 1939. Gas lighting gave way to electricity, the wireless set gave the latest news, and more and more homes had telephones; but the many improvements in ordinary life were overshadowed by unemployment and the threat of war.

When war came, it brought much destruction. The railways and factories immediately to the north of Clapham were major targets in bombing raids. In many streets the place a bomb dropped is marked by a post-war block of flats in a gap in the Victorian terraces. There was a major anti-aircraft gun emplacement on the Common, as well as allotments and prefabs as temporary housing. Beneath the Northern Line deep shelters were built.

In the darkest days of the war politicians and planners were looking ahead to a better society. John Battley, a local printer who in 1945 became the first Labour MP for Clapham, had a vision of a new Clapham, substantially rebuilt with well-designed flats and labour-saving houses. The flats should be interspersed with public gardens, and there should be good shopping and good public facilities – cinema, theatre, library, baths, schools, institutes, public halls. **After the War**, there was much rebuilding, but never the resources nor indeed the will to carry through what now seems a utopian vision. The Clapham of those years was a shabby and unattractive place, with a poor reputation, where taxi drivers north of the River were notoriously reluctant to go.

John Battley and his wife, Sybil. 1933

Attempts to produce a planned environment continued and peaked after most of Clapham became part of the London Borough of Lambeth in 1965. The need to conserve our built heritage had been accepted since the 1940s, but only the better parts, and much of the older fabric was still seen by the planners as having outlived its usefulness. Planning laws and developmental policies were also hostile to the workshops and smaller factories which were still a part of residential areas. More and more were driven out, or faced by rising rentals gave up, and apart from a few clusters often around the railway arches, Clapham provided less and less manual employment. **From the mid-1970s** the tide was running strongly in favour of preservation and rehabilitation of the older housing stock. Appreciation of Victorian buildings and reaction against the suburban life-style, in favour of urban living, brought Clapham back into favour as a place for the well-off to live. Soaring house prices brought about a rapid social transformation, so that by the end of the century Clapham was a place for the rich and smart, side by side with people living in serious social deprivation. The value of land for housing provided an incentive to build on any spare space. Local employment was now mainly in the service industries, many housed in older buildings which had found new uses. The expansion of London's population has always been driven by immigrants. Those who have found their way to Clapham have included Huguenots and other refugees from the Continent. In the nineteenth and early twentieth centuries Irish and Welsh people came looking for work; the Irish contributed to the Roman Catholic revival, and the Welsh built their chapel at Clapham Junction. During the Second World War Polish servicemen and refugees arrived, and after the war Africans and Afro-Caribbeans. Refugees have included Vietnamese and people fleeing from strife in the Balkans. Modern Clapham is visibly and audibly a multi-ethnic and multi-lingual society.

We have come a long way from the little Saxon village. The authors of this book hope that our descriptions of Clapham past will help our understanding of Clapham present and to come.

St Paul's Church

The original village of Clapham was centred around the area of St Paul's Church in Rectory Grove. The village church, then called Holy Trinity, stood on the site of the present church. Medieval in origin, the church had various additions during the sixteenth to eighteenth centuries, but as the population of Clapham grew the old church became too small and a new Holy Trinity Church was built on Clapham Common in the 1770s.

Most of the old church was destroyed, leaving only a chapel for funerals, pictured here, prior to its demolition to make way for a new church. This church, now called St Paul's, was built in 1815 to relieve the pressure on the already overcrowded Holy Trinity on the Common and to serve the inhabitants of the new streets then being built on former farmland in the east of the parish. St Paul's is a plain rectangular Georgian *'preaching box'*, with no tower, which was built at a modest cost of £5,000. But it is remarkable for the rich collection of monuments which were salvaged from the old church. The finest of these is the monument of the Atkins family, once the

The old Parish Church: the surviving north aisle shortly before its demolition. Engraving by Bartholomew Howlett, 1815

Lords of the Manor. This is a group of three children of Sir Richard Atkins, all of whom had predeceased their parents. Before his own death in 1689 Sir Richard commissioned the group from the sculptor, William Stanton. On a tomb chest, which originally stood in front of this group, are effigies of Sir Richard and Lady Atkins by the same sculptor. When the old church was demolished the monument was consigned to a vault, where it was forgotten until a local historian, J W Grover, discovered it in 1886 and re-erected it in the church.

There is also a monument to William Hewer, clerk and later good friend of Samuel Pepys. The oldest memorial is a brass to William Tableer, who died in 1401, while others commemorated include the bookseller, John Hatchard.

The church was well restored in the 1970s when the chancel, which had been added in 1879, was cut off to provide a community space. The original galleries had been removed earlier.

In the churchyard many gravestones have been destroyed, but tombs of some notable local families such as the Thorntons and the Hibberts can still be found, as well as that of the sculptor, Sir Henry Cheere. From the north side of the churchyard there is a splendid view over the adjoining allotments, down towards the river and right across London to Big Ben and the London Eye. This view reminds us of the prime location of the medieval village in its raised position above the road from London to Kingston.

The small square in front of the church is flanked on one side by pretty eighteenth century houses including the one where Zachary Macaulay first set up his African Academy. On the other side the low buildings adjoining Ingleton House were built as a hall and chapel for a boys' school in 1913.

The Atkins monument, by William Stanton. This group, of the three children of Sir Richard and Lady Atkins who predeceased their parents, was erected by Sir Richard before his death in 1689

The Manor House

Near the village church stood the Manor House. The small moated medieval house grew over the centuries. In the reign of Elizabeth I the manor was bought by Bartholomew Clerke, a lawyer, courtier and diplomat, who added a large mansion in the style of the day. The Queen dined there in 1583 on her way to Greenwich. Dr Henry Atkins, physician to James I, acquired the house in 1616 and it remained in the family for several generations.

In 1629 it was described as *'a faire Mansion House of Bricke with faire Hall, Parlor, and Dining Chamber well wainscoated, a good Kitchen, Brewhouse, and Washhouse served with water in Leaden Pipes, a larder, good Selleridge, and other convenient houses of office with good Barne, Stable, and dovehouse and good Orchard, and gardens well walled, and set with all manner of good fruit, and water coming into them in Pipes of Leade'*.

In the mid-eighteenth century the Manor House became a boarding school for young ladies, and later for boys, which it remained until it was demolished in 1837 to make way for the houses of Turret Grove and adjoining streets. The name of Turret Grove derives from the domed turret which originally surmounted the octagonal tower at one end of the Manor House, but contemporary illustrations show that this was removed at some time prior to the demolition of the house.

The grounds of the Manor House extended as far as Wandsworth Road and contained six fishponds. A coat of arms which can now be seen on No. 12 Old Town is reputed to have come from the old Manor House.

The Manor House, Clapham about 1830. Lithograph by an unknown artist

Hibberts' Almshouses

Before continuing up towards Old Town it is worth diverting to Wandsworth Road to look at the delightful terrace of almshouses built in Gothic style by local architect, Edward I'Anson. An inscription on a tablet in the central pediment reads: *'These houses for eight aged women were erected by Sarah Hibbert and Mary Ann Hibbert in grateful remembrance of their father William Hibbert, Esq., long an inhabitant of Clapham anno domini 1859'.*

William Hibbert was a West India merchant who lived on Clapham Common South Side in a house, now demolished, which stood at the corner of Crescent Lane. He had seven children, and these two daughters, who both remained single, were prolific diarists. They travelled extensively in Britain and Europe and many volumes of their unpublished diaries survive.

William's brother George was also a Clapham resident with a large house and garden on North Side. He too was a West India merchant and a notable collector of plants, which he imported for his Clapham garden.

The almshouses each had a kitchen and living room on the ground floor with a bedroom above and a tiny garden behind. Bathrooms were not added until the 1950s. In the 1980s the houses were renovated and modernised. They are a most attractive addition to the streetscape of Wandsworth Road.

Hibberts' Almshouses, Nos. 715–729 Wandsworth Road. Probably an architect's drawing, 1860

Clapham Old School

From the Manor House the old main street of the village, once called just The Street, winds up to the former village school. In a deed of 1648 the Lord of the Manor, Sir Richard Atkins, granted to the inhabitants of Clapham '*for ever the School and School-house which they or some other benefactors had built at their own costs and charges upon part of the waste of the manor*'.

The former Parochial School building in Rectory Grove

At first it appears to have been a grammar school, where the three Rs were taught as well as Latin and Greek and '*accompts*', but it later became a free charity school for young children. Early nineteenth-century illustrations show the octagonal school house, as rebuilt by voluntary subscription in 1809, where the older boys are teaching the younger ones.

As the population grew, more classrooms were needed. In 1838 the trustees were given some new ground in Macaulay Road to erect a school '*for poor children of the parish*'. The boys were transferred to that building (now converted to a private house) while the girls remained in Rectory Grove. New buildings were added from 1852 onwards, and in 1877 the octagon was replaced by the classroom on the Old Town side of the present building.

The school was known as Clapham Parochial School until in 1950 it was renamed Macaulay School. By that time, all infants' classes were in the Rectory Grove building, and it was not until 1965 when the present Macaulay School in Victoria Rise was completed that the school was united on one site. The oldest of several foundation stones and the quill pen weather-vane were transferred from Rectory Grove to the school in Victoria Rise.

The Rectory Grove building passed to Lambeth Council and has at various times been used for remedial teaching.

Sycamore House

Soon after the old school the fine double-fronted Sycamore House can be seen on the right. This house was built in 1787 and remained a private residence until the 1840s when, like many other large Clapham houses, it became a school. In 1898 Alexander Denis Leman acquired it as the base for his expanding Sycamore Laundry.

The business was started in 1865 by a Mrs Buckland who took in washing for the local gentry. Her daughter married a wholesale tobacconist, Mr Leman, who decided to take over the thriving laundry business, and as it grew he moved it to these premises. Gradually the laundry works were built over the extensive gardens behind Sycamore House. On Alexander's death his two sons, and then his grandsons, ran the business until the family business finally merged in 1994 with Blossom and Browne.

The Royal warrants on Sycamore Laundry, No. 4 Old Town, 1978

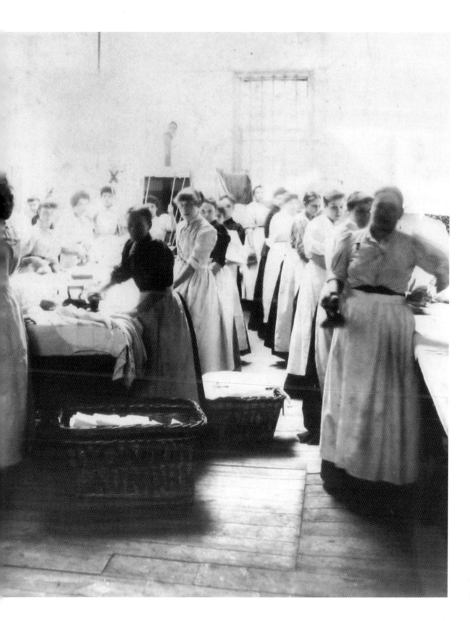

Over the years the Sycamore Laundry acquired a very high reputation and received royal warrants from the Queen, the Duke of Edinburgh, the late Queen Mother and the Prince of Wales. These were formerly proudly displayed over the porch of Sycamore House.

At the time of the merger a small shop (No. 8) was retained for taking in laundry which is now sent elsewhere in London. Sycamore House was converted to flats and the works behind were demolished for the building of a gated development, Sycamore Mews. The extent of the mews indicates how large the laundry works had become.

Women workers in the laundry, late nineteenth century

39-43 Old Town

These three Queen Anne houses, built in 1707 by Daniel Clarke, are some of the most important to survive in Clapham. They have retained much of their original architectural detail, including the wooden eaves cornice and the doorways with wooden pilasters, and the houses have been well restored and maintained in recent years. Even some of the original interior wooden panelling survives.

A blue plaque on No. 43 records that this was once the home of J F Bentley, the architect of Westminster Cathedral, and it is said that on a clear day he could see the tower of the cathedral from his house. J F Bentley was also responsible for the Monastery and the Lady Chapel and some light fittings and stained glass at St Mary's Church in Clapham Park Road, where he was a regular member of the congregation. He added a rear extension to his Old Town house and designed oak furniture for his dining room. Bentley was a noted collector of blue and white oriental china and of Venetian glass.

These houses originally had long gardens stretching as far as the gardens of the Grafton Square houses behind. In the 1930s part of the gardens were built on by a printing works, which later became the home of the printers, Battley Brothers. In 1945 the founder of the firm, John Battley, was elected as the first Labour Member of Parliament for Clapham. When Battley Brothers moved to larger premises in Battersea in 2003 the factory was replaced by housing.

J F Bentley, architect.
Painting by W C Symons, 1902

Decorated doorcase of No. 39 Old Town

Grafton Square

In the eighteenth century a large mansion stood in extensive grounds on this site. At different times it was the home of various important families, but notably of the wealthy Thornton Astell family. The house was demolished in the 1840s when Thomas Ross acquired the land to develop the tall terraced houses of Grafton Square. Their elaborate stucco decorations with elongated trumpet shapes beside the windows and rosette friezes are very unusual and distinctive. There are similar decorations on some houses nearby in Rectory Grove, which must have been built by Ross at about the same time.

Ross incorporated a short terrace of earlier houses (Nos. 1-3) and only completed just over two sides of his projected square before building stopped, presumably because the project was not as successful as he had hoped. He was among those who pressed for a railway through Clapham, at a time when property developers believed that a local station would be to their benefit.

On the south-west corner of the square, opposite The Polygon and near The Sun pub, a large Congregational Church was built in 1851. This was badly damaged in the Second World War and was replaced by the present church which became the United Reformed Church, but has now passed into other hands. The minister at the Congregational Church for many years was Dr Guinness Rogers, a notable preacher and a friend of the Prime Minister William Gladstone, who used to visit Rogers at his house on North Side.

A Baptist Chapel was built in the 1880s on the empty site on the north-west corner. The chapel later became the People's Church, which was sold in 2004 and has now been converted for residential use. The garden in the centre of Grafton Square was originally private with lawns, shrubs and flowers in large stone pots. In the 1930s it was a tennis club and is now a public open space with a children's playground.

The site at the end of the southern terrace of Grafton Square, on the corner of Old Town, has been empty for many years since some buildings were destroyed after bomb damage in the Second World War. At one time there was a plan for a police station here, but that was abandoned in favour of a large residential development.

Dr and Mrs Guinness Rogers, around 1880

Houses on the east side of Grafton Square

The Polygon

This curiously shaped block of buildings, appropriately named to reflect its shape, dates from the late eighteenth century. The least altered part of the original development is the corner shop, now the office of Palace Estates. This was once the premises of E Durham, Bottle Merchant and Grocer, and the large pitchers which marked his shop can still be seen at first floor level. The shop remained in use by a grocer until the 1980s and has retained its shopfront almost unchanged.

The Rose and Crown pub has had additions and alterations at various times although it too is basically eighteenth century. Some of the early houses also survive in good original condition at the other end of The Polygon facing on to Clapham Common.

The Polygon was badly damaged by bombing in the Second World War and most of the side facing The Pavement was occupied by a second-hand car dealer for many years, before being rebuilt in the early twenty-first century in sympathetic style to complete the ensemble.

No. 1 The Polygon, when it was a grocery and Post Office, 1978

24

Old Fire Station

This was once the site of the village lock-up where thieves, drunks and vagrants were locked up for the night by the watchman. In the same position a single storey fire-engine house was built, probably in the 1840s, for the Clapham Fire Brigade. In those days the address of the man who had the key was displayed on a notice-board outside and when there was a fire he had to be summoned while the volunteer firemen were roused.

The fire station was taken over by the London Fire Brigade in 1867 and it was decided that a new station should be built. The present Gothic building, designed by the architect to the Fire Brigade, Edward Cresy, and built at a cost of £615, was opened in 1869. A new, larger, fire station was built in Old Town in 1902 in the exact location of the present one. Bob Pethurst who lived in The Polygon as a child in the early 1900s recalled the old building before it closed: *'looking through the huge doors, you could see a row of about eight brass helmets and a wonderful fire engine. I used to get a great thrill to see the fire engine pulled along by two white horses. I think that's because the turnout was so spectacular.... When the fire engine was motorised it was still a wonderful sight, with the firemen hanging on. I can recall the thump of the solid rubber tyres on the bumpy roads. It fair shook our house'.*

After the opening of the new building, the Old Fire Station was used by the local council as a residence for the officer in charge of the Common, and for other service purposes. It was sold for private residential use in 2005.

The Old Fire Station, Old Town

17 The Pavement

This is the finest surviving early shop front in Clapham. Not only is the exterior of the shop much as it was originally built, but some of the early shopfittings – glass cases and solid wooden shelves – are still in use in the present gift shop. These were built for the chemist, Henry Deane, who took over the shop from a grocer in 1837. Large coloured glass bottles with the names of various medicines in gold lettering once lined the shelves. These remained long after Henry Deane's death, as the shop was a chemist's until the mid-1980s.

The entrance to the shop was in the centre and a door to the right of the building gave access to the first floor living room and the upper floors where the family and shop assistants slept. There is a particularly attractive cast iron balcony to the first floor. The painted sign high up on the southern flank wall of the building has also survived in remarkably good condition.

Henry Deane was a noted pharmacist and became President of the recently formed Pharmaceutical Society in 1853. He was also a keen photographer and his pictures taken in the 1850s and 1860s provide an unrivalled visual record of Clapham at the time, and have frequently been reproduced in local publications.

No. 17 The Pavement, Deanes the Chemists (now Zeitgeist), 1976

26

Holy Trinity Church

Holy Trinity Church, Clapham Common

During the eighteenth century, as merchants leaving central London started to build large houses around the open space of Clapham Common, the hub of Clapham moved from the original village around the parish church, on the site of the present St Paul's, up to the Common. The old church was too small, inconvenient and run down and it was decided that a new church was needed.

An Act of Parliament was required to build the new church on common land. This was duly passed and Holy Trinity Church was built in 1774–76 to a design by the architect Kenton Couse, who had recently completed the rebuilding of the frontage of No. 10 Downing Street. The simple classical plan is that of a preaching box, and the interior was dominated by a large, finely carved three-tier pulpit, which was later altered, so that only part now survives. There were galleries on three sides, which survive, and box pews, which do not. The belfry, with a small lead dome and gilded cross, houses the original clock supplied by Thwaites of Clerkenwell.

Alterations, including a new porch added in 1812 to give shelter to those alighting from their carriages, were made as a result of the large crowds attracted by the preaching of the Rector, John Venn. Other alterations at various times reflect the changes in approach to worship. In the early twentieth century the church was extended to the east and the original apse replaced by the present chancel.

The east window was moved to the Lady Chapel, which was converted into the Wilberforce Centre in the early 1990s. At that time too the west end of the church was screened off under the gallery and a central altar platform created.

John Venn was a champion of the poor and needy, responsible for welfare and educational reforms locally, and he was also a leading figure in the Clapham Sect.

The Revd. John Venn, Rector 1792-1813. Engraving after a drawing by Joseph Slater, 1813

Holy Trinity Church has become well-known for its connections with the Clapham Sect, which was not a 'sect' in its true sense, but a group of local businessmen, most of whom worshipped at the church, who campaigned vigourously for the abolition of the slave trade.

The members included William Wilberforce, Henry Thornton, Zachary Macaulay and Granville Sharp, who all lived around Clapham Common.

A stone plaque listing the names of the members of the Clapham Sect and commemorating their achievements can be seen on the south wall of Holy Trinity Church. This plaque was damaged by a Second World War bomb in 1945, and has been left in its damaged state. A blue plaque was put up in 1983 on the 150th anniversary of the death of William Wilberforce. The benefactors' boards inside the entrance recording the names of donors to needy parishioners include those of Samuel Pepys' clerk, William Hewer and the widow of the explorer Captain Cook.

The Library

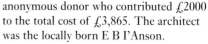

Public libraries were an innovation of the later nineteenth century. London was slower to adopt these than the provinces; when Clapham Library was opened in 1889, it was one of only seventeen in the London County Council area, ten of them first proposed in 1887.

The initiative came from three local people, a vicar, a churchwarden and an anonymous donor who contributed £2000 to the total cost of £3,865. The architect was the locally born E B I'Anson.

As built the library had a reading room and a reference room downstairs; upstairs was a meeting room and the librarian's living accommodation. The upstairs room later became a reference library and then a study room, while the downstairs was opened out.

Outside the library is a Roman altar stone which was removed to this site from the grounds of Cavendish House on South Side, when the house was demolished to build the streets to the south of Cavendish Road. The early history of the stone is uncertain but it is thought to have come to Clapham from the Tower of London some time in the eighteenth or nineteenth century.

E B I'Anson was the son of Edward I'Anson (architect of Hibberts' Almshouses and the Alexandra Hotel) a distinguished City of London commercial architect and estate surveyor. The I'Ansons lived in Clapham from the 1840s to the 1870s and took part in the activities of the parish.

Clapham Library, Clapham Common North Side

George West House

This building was originally a factory for Ross Ensign Limited, manufacturers of lenses and optical equipment. The company had been on this site since the 1890s, but a modern factory was built during the First World War in an effort to extend in Britain key industries which had in the past been dominated by Germany. It survived as a successful company until after the Second World War, when it finally succumbed to competition from a revived Germany and Japan.

The company closed on this site in 1973, and for many years the building was used as offices by, among others, Lambeth Council who named it George West House after a local councillor.

In 1998 the expanding computer software company, QAS (Quick Address Systems) which had started in Clapham a few years earlier, purchased the building and hired architects, Allies & Morrison, to adapt it. The interior was stripped to make large open plan offices with a central staircase running from the ground floor reception area to the third floor lunchroom. The result is a very light and airy interior. Two glass pavilions were added on the roof, from which there are panoramic views over London. The exterior was cleaned and restored, a new stone-dressed ramp and stairway made to the entrance portico, the railings and gates reinstated and the original clock overhauled.

Roof terrace of George West House,
No. 4 Clapham Common North Side, 2003

Church Buildings

This fine terrace is among the earliest surviving buildings in Clapham. It was constructed between 1714-20 by John Hutt, senior, whose initials appear over the bricked up archway of No. 14, together with the date of completion and the date of the expiry of the 199-year lease (1913). The original iron railings and gates survive and are listed Grade II* as is the terrace itself.

When the original lease expired the terrace was purchased by the Westminster Hospital, with a view to rebuilding the hospital on this site. However, the First World War intervened and the plan was shelved indefinitely. The houses became very dilapidated and were due to be demolished by a speculator when, as a result of an appeal made by the Society for the Preservation of Ancient Buildings in 1933, several purchasers were found who undertook to restore the houses. By this time the houses at the west end of the row had already been demolished and the blocks of flats, Woodlands and Okeover Manor, built in 1934 and 1935. At the same time the cottages and stables behind were sold to the London County Council and replaced by the flats in Macaulay Road.

Nos. 15-17 were gutted and made into a single block of flats in 1935 and No. 14 was seriously damaged by fire in 1955. The house was rebuilt, but the arch which originally lead to the out-buildings behind was bricked up.

Several well-known people have lived in this terrace. No. 13, which has a bay window added around 1830 and fine oak panelling, was once the home of the distinguished eighteenth century collector of books and prints, Revd. C M Cracherode. The novelist, Graham Greene, lived at No. 14 and set his wartime novel *The End of the Affair* in Clapham. The same house was once a school attended by Thomas Babington Macaulay, and the home of Granville Sharp, a member of the Clapham Sect.

Old buildings behind Clapham Common North Side, sketch by Victoria Belcher, 1932

Church Buildings, Clapham Common North Side

Trinity Hospice

The hospice, which occupies four adjoining buildings, Nos. 29-32 North Side, was founded in 1891 as the Free Home for the Dying. It was later renamed the Hostel of God and following a major reorganisation in 1977 when the nuns who had previously run it were replaced by a lay council, and the buildings were renovated to comply with new health regulations, it became Trinity Hospice. A single storey ward, added behind in 1953, is to be demolished in 2006 to build a modern extension. The gardens of Trinity Hospice were restored from 1981 onwards by John Medhurst, following the principles and in memory of the American born landscape gardener, Lanning Roper. The garden is divided into several distinct areas of interest. Sweeping lawns, paths, raised beds and a brick loggia are divided from a wild area by a high hedge. In an ovoid shaped pond is a rotating stainless steel sculpture by George Rickey, and in another pond a curved miniature waterfall is by local sculptor, William Pye. The gardens are regularly opened to the public.

The most striking of the houses is No. 29, once called The Elms, which is in simple classical style, and still has its original staircase with turned balusters and marble fireplaces in the ground floor rooms. The stable block behind was converted into a chapel in 1933. An early occupant of this house was Robert Barclay of the banking family, a keen astronomer, who built an observatory in his garden. A later occupant was the architect of the Houses of Parliament, Sir Charles Barry (1795-1860), who is commemorated with a blue plaque.

No. 31, formerly called The Hollies, was once the home of the architect J T Knowles, junior who founded the *Nineteenth Century* magazine and was a close friend of Lord Tennyson.

Towards the back of the hospice garden, and on a site now cut through by The Chase, once stood the most important house in Clapham. This was built in 1663 by Sir Denis Gauden, and in that year the diarist Samuel Pepys made the first of several visits, which he described in his diary. The house was later bought by Pepys' friend William Hewer, and Pepys came to live here in 1700 when he left his central London home because of ill health. He died in Clapham in 1703.

Sadly, no picture of the house is known, but according to a contemporary record *'it formed three sides of a square, the principal front looking to the Common. Some of the rooms were wainscoted in japan and a spacious gallery occupied the whole length of the house above and below stairs'.*

Samuel Pepys. Ivory medallion carved by Jean Cavalier, 1688

The Elms, No. 29 Clapham Common North Side

Cedars Terraces

The very large and striking buildings which flank Cedars Road were built in French Renaissance style by the local architect J T Knowles junior in 1860. The original plan was that they would form the gateway to a huge development by Knowles to be known as Park Town, which would stretch as far as the river. However, the scheme was never wholly realised, partly because the building of the railway lines running from Victoria to Clapham Junction across the lower part of the site made the area less attractive. Large detached houses were built on Cedars Road, but most of these were demolished in the late 1940s as a result of war damage.

The two blocks dominate the view even from the far side of the Common, and are a very assertive Clapham landmark. Each terrace comprises five separate houses, the three centre ones with five storeys and the house at each end with an extra storey in the roof pavilion. The houses in the eastern terrace have mostly been divided into flats, while the western terrace has been a hostel for many years, but is now due for conversion to flats.

Much of the original elaborate and distinctive decoration to the balconies and the window heads survives. Similar decorations can be seen on some of the houses in Cedars Road and even further down Queenstown Road where a few of Knowles's proposed houses were built. The predominant ivy-leaf motif can also be seen on a fragment of the garden wall which survives at the top of the west side of Cedars Road. The first floor drawing room of No. 45 was lavishly

John Hatchard

Edvard and Nina Grieg in Clapham, 1888

A house which once stood near the present Wix's Lane, next to that of the Wix family who gave their name to the street, was the home of John Hatchard (1768-1849) the bookseller of Piccadilly.

After working for a well-known antiquarian bookseller John Hatchard set up his own business in Piccadilly in 1797 at the age of 28 with capital of £5. The business flourished and became the most famous bookshop in London, patronised by Queen Charlotte and other members of the Royal Family.

The shop was rather like a club, and William Wilberforce used a room there for his anti-slavery meetings and had his mail delivered there. The first meeting of the Royal Horticultural Society was held at Hatchards in 1815.

After living above the shop for many years, John Hatchard and his family moved to Stonely House on Clapham Common North Side in 1821, where he spent the rest of his life.

He was a generous philanthropist, supporting and leaving money to many good causes including the church and schools in Clapham. He apparently often dressed in black, in a coat in the style of a bishop's frock coat, with a waistcoat buttoned to the throat and knee breeches and gaiters.

There is a memorial to John Hatchard in St Paul's Church, Rectory Grove but he is buried at St James's Church in Park Hill, in a vault which survived the destruction of the church by bombing in the Second World War. Hatchard's most lasting memorial is the Piccadilly bookshop, which retains his name, though there is no longer a family connection.

*John Hatchard.
Painting by Henry Wyatt,
1826*

decorated, with scagliola columns, mirror panelled doors and extensive gilding.

The house on the eastern corner of Cedars Road, No. 47, was the home of the music publisher George Augener (1830-1915) who was London agent of the Norwegian composer, Edvard Grieg (1843-1907). Grieg and his wife frequently stayed here on their visits to London, when the Norwegian flag was flown from the house. A blue plaque was erected in 2004 to commemorate these visits.

No. 47 Clapham Common North Side

Eaton House The Manor

The main house of the present school was one of the large private houses built around the Common at the end of the eighteenth century. It was called Byrom House, later known as The Beeches, and was once famous for its fine gardens and golden pheasants. The present buildings have been an educational establishment for just one hundred years.

In 1876 Dr F C Maxwell founded Manor House School in Clapham Old Town. His eldest son, Stanley Maxwell, who succeeded his father as headmaster in 1898, moved the school to Clapham Common North Side in 1906. It was then that the red brick side extension was built to accommodate the rapidly growing, successful school.

Stanley Maxwell, who ran the school for 40 years, was a leading proponent of the value of independent schools and for 30 years Chairman of the Private (later Independent) Schools Association. His brother Donald was an official First World War artist, who wrote and illustrated over 30 volumes himself as well as illustrating books for many other authors including those of another brother, Gordon, who was also a prolific writer.

The family lived here and ran the school until 1938, when Stanley Maxwell retired. Among the distinguished pupils at the school were the sculptor, Maurice Lambert (1901-1964) and briefly also his brother the composer Constant Lambert (1905-1951). Battersea College, which later became part of South Bank Polytechnic, took over the buildings after the closure of Manor House School.

In due course changes in further education led to the closure of the college and the premises were bought by Eaton House Schools, who opened a boys' preparatory school here in 1993. The earlier school is recalled by the present name, Eaton House The Manor.

In 2005 a major extension was built to provide a new wing by filling in a courtyard behind the school and a third floor was added to the 1906 extension, which the Maxwell family had providently constructed with footings and foundations designed to take an extra storey.

Manor House School,
No. 58 Clapham Common North Side
from a drawing by Donald Maxwell, around 1920

Gilmore House

In 1763 Isaac Ackerman of Battersea Rise House, which stood in extensive grounds roughly behind the present Nos. 115-120 Clapham Common West Side, built a pair of houses which were intended to frame the view from his house towards the hills of north London. These were known as The Sisters houses.

In 1895 the eastern of the two houses was demolished to build a new smaller house, Alverstoke, and Sisters Avenue. The remaining house took the name Gilmore House from Mrs. Gilmore, who founded the Anglican Order of Deaconesses which was based here. Mrs Gilmore was the sister of William Morris, whose friend the architect Philip Webb designed a small chapel for her at the rear of the house in 1897. The stained glass windows of the chapel were made by Morris & Co. to designs by Edward Burne-Jones. All the fittings and furnishings – altar table, pews, cross, lectern – were also designed by the architect. The chapel survives, though stripped of its furnishings, some of which are in the Victoria & Albert Museum.

A blue plaque on the building commemorates the fact that from 1773 to 1781 this was the home of the founder of *The Times* newspaper, John Walter (1739-1812). There have been various additions and alterations to the building, including an unsightly 1980s projection into the front garden. The busts on the exterior are of Milton and Shakespeare.

Gilmore House,
No. 113 Clapham Common North Side

The Shrubbery

Marie Stillman.
Photograph by Julia Margaret Cameron, 1868

In Lavender Gardens hidden by St Barnabas' Church on North Side is a splendid Georgian mansion, the grounds of which once stretched from Clapham Common to the Kingston Road, now Lavender Hill. The house was built in 1796 for a wealthy city merchant and Lord Mayor of London, George Scholey, and was occupied by his son until the 1840s. The next owner, John Humphery, who was the owner of Hay's Wharf on the south bank of the Port of London and pro-Reform MP for Southwark, also became Lord Mayor. He almost doubled the size of the house, adding a ballroom, a 30-metre long state drawing room, a dining room and a large circular drawing room. The house also had ten bedrooms, four dressing rooms on the first floor, and six rooms on the top floor for servants.

A later resident was the Greek merchant, Michael Spartali, whose two beautiful daughters, Christina and Marie, were models for painters including Whistler, Burne-Jones and Rossetti and for the photographer Julia Margaret Cameron. Marie was a notable artist herself under her married name of Marie Stillman.

The Shrubbery from Clapham Common North Side. Lithograph by an unknown artist, 1885

The Spartali family left the house in the late 1880s and since no private buyer was found the house became a girls' school, while the grounds were sold to develop the streets down to Lavender Hill and St Barnabas' Church was built on the front lawn in 1898 by a local architect, W Bassett Smith. The interior of this large Gothic-style church was remodelled in the 1990s to provide community facilities at the west end.

When the school closed The Shrubbery became the vicarage for a while and then the church hall, but was eventually divided up and then fell into disuse. After some war damage, and many years of neglect and near dereliction, the building was finally restored and converted into quality flats in 1987.

Some internal features have been lost over the years but much of interest still remains in the sensitive conversion. The black and white marble entrance hall with scagliola columns and the stone staircase with iron balustrades have been restored and the main rooms have fortunately escaped being divided into small units.

3 – Around the High Street

St Anne's Hall, Venn Street

The date plaque over the door to the side entrance in Bromells Road records that St Anne's Hall was built in 1895. The architect was a local man, E B I'Anson, who was also responsible for the library on North Side and for the former art school in Edgeley Road (now Pearson Mews).

The hall was built by Holy Trinity Church as a mission building, and originally included a dispensary and a soup kitchen entered by the side door to the left of the building in Bromells Road. In the basement there was a working men's club; the club had previously been at St Anne's House in Old Town and brought the name to the new building. This was all part of a major redevelopment at the end of the nineteenth century of this area just off the High Street, which at the time was a warren of little courtyards and alleyways lined with wooden clapboard cottages and shops. St Anne's Hall is now used as a community centre.

The Postmen's Office, now the Royal Mail Sorting Office, just along the road was part of the same development, built in 1902 as shown on the decorated plaque along with the royal coat of arms.

In 1910 the Electric Picture Palace, one of several early picture houses in Clapham, opened on the site of the present Clapham Picture House. Nine years later adjoining buildings were bought and a new enlarged cinema to be called the Coliseum was planned and building started. However, the company ran into financial difficulties and the cinema never opened. Part of the

St Anne's House and Hall, the entrance facing Bromells Road

grandiose scheme can still be seen in the faience façade above the shop on the corner of Venn Street and the High Street.

For years the building was put to various uses, finishing as a snooker hall before it was converted and re-opened as a cinema in 1992. The proposed Coliseum would have seated 3000 people in one auditorium, with an orchestra pit and a tea room seating 140 people. Today, the Clapham Picture House, which was enlarged in 1999 has four screens and a licensed café-bar.

Museum of British Transport,
Clapham High Street, 1963

I n 1885 a horse tram depot opened in Clapham High Street with a narrow entrance between shops. One of the shops became another of Clapham's early picture houses, The Globe, which opened in 1910. This little cinema, seating only 130, closed in 1915 when there were already several other cinemas in Clapham High Street. The tram depot was rebuilt and extended in 1904 for electric trams, which entered from Clapham High Street and exited into Clapham Park Road.

During the Second World War, in April 1941, the depot was seriously damaged by bombing. After the war it was rebuilt as a bus garage, but this closed in 1958 and the Museum of British Transport opened in

the same building in 1960. In its collection were *Mallard*, the steam locomotive which held the world speed record, royal coaches from the nineteenth century and a wide range of London buses and trams.

This was a major local attraction and the proposed closure in the early 1970s was fiercely resisted. However, the museum finally closed in 1973 when the collection was dispersed – some to London Transport who opened their own museum in Covent Garden a few years later, and some to the National Railway Museum in York.

The redundant building was put to various uses – it was a bus garage again for a few years and then a go-karting track – before it was bought by Sainsbury's and demolished together with three adjoining houses for the present supermarket. This building, designed by Chetwood Associates, was opened in 1999. The original design included a novel 17m by 2.5m video wall, made up of 20 screens and intended to advertise products. This was not successful since the pictures were frequently made invisible by reflection and strong sunlight, so it was soon replaced by the present shop window.

Clapham Tram Depot
destroyed by bombing in April 1941.
Note the spire of St Mary's Church
in the background

Some High Street Residents

Among some notable former residents of Clapham High Street was Mrs Elizabeth Cook, widow of the explorer Captain James Cook. There is a tradition that Captain Cook himself lived on Clapham Common North Side and that he planted three trees on the Common before setting out on his final voyage. This is legend; the trees were probably planted by his eldest son, also a naval captain; but his widow did live in Clapham from 1788 until her death at the age of 94 in 1835.

For twenty years she shared her house with her cousin, Admiral Isaac Smith, who as a young midshipman had accompanied Captain Cook on the *Endeavour* and was said to be the first European to have set foot in Australia. Mrs Cook left legacies to several local families and a gift to six poor widows, as is recorded on a benefactors' board in Holy Trinity Church.

Clapham Grammar School occupied a prime position on the High Street in the nineteenth century – some remains of the chapel, now in commercial use, can still be seen at the end of Carpenters Place. The Revd. Charles Pritchard, the founder and headmaster of the school, built it into a successful establishment to which pupils were attracted from some distance; amongst them were the sons of the astronomer Sir John Herschel and Charles Darwin. Pritchard himself was a distinguished astronomer. He had a small observatory at the school and when he retired became Professor of Astronomy at Oxford.

Clapham Terrace (now much altered as Nos. 24–36 Clapham High Street) was once a fashionable address. Robert Barclay, the brewer lived there, while his cousin and name-sake Robert Barclay the banker lived at No. 29 North Side. Other residents included John Thornton, grandson of John Thornton of the Clapham Sect, with his novelist wife, Elizabeth, and the campaigner for cathedral choristers, Maria Hackett.

Elizabeth Cook, widow of Captain James Cook. Painting by W Henderson, 1830

Revd. Charles Pritchard, founder and headmaster of Clapham Grammar School, around 1860

Clapham Manor Street

This was one of the earlier streets of Clapham to be developed. In 1827 a few houses already existed at the High Street end of the road and the following year Thomas Cubitt took a lease on some land in the middle of the street. It was some years before he started developing the land, and he gradually leased and built on more land so that by the mid-1850s both sides of the street were lined with charming early Victorian houses.

Although several houses were demolished to build Clapham Manor Estate in the 1970s most remaining houses have been well restored and maintained. The imposing building on the west of the street towards Larkhall Rise was built as the charitable Clapham Dispensary. It was designed, free of charge, by the local architect J T Knowles senior, the father of the Knowles who designed the Cedars Terraces (Chapter 2). It was built (1850-54) by public subscription on land given by the ground landlord, Major Atkins Bowyer. Thomas Cubitt paid 25 guineas annually to this charitable foundation. The building has been put to various uses since the dispensary closed and it now houses a centre for ballet and exercise classes as well as a taxi drivers' school.

The Bread and Roses, originally called The Bowyer Arms, and the adjoining houses date from 1846-52 and are the only buildings in the street built by Thomas Cubitt himself. When the pub was acquired by the Workers Beer Company in 1996

The Bread and Roses, Clapham Manor Street, originally The Bowyer Arms

Claud Butler, King of the Lightweights, from a catalogue, 1939

CLAUD BUTLER—
the man you are dealing with

it was renamed using the title of a song written during a strike of female textile workers in Massachusetts in 1912.

Clapham Leisure Centre was opened as Clapham Public Baths in July 1932 by Prince George, later the Duke of Kent. The swimming pool (approximately 30m long by 11m wide) was surrounded on three sides by teak *'dressing boxes'* which could be folded back to form a panelled partition between the *'bath hall'* and the corridor in winter when the swimming pool was covered with a sprung maple floor for dancing. There were also club rooms, a buffet, kitchen and store on the first floor, as well as shower and slipper baths for both men and women. The area occupied by the latter is now the fitness centre.

The building was on a one-acre site with frontages to Clapham Manor Street and Voltaire Road and access to Edgeley Road at the rear. The baths have suffered from neglect over the years and in 2006 plans to relocate them became a major issue in the elections to Lambeth Council.

Among the small businesses in this street in the 1930s was Claud Butler, *'maker of lightweight racing and touring bicycles, tandems and tricycles'* known as *'King of Lightweights'*, whose bicycles are still much-prized today.

The Former Temperance Billiard Hall

The distinctive barrel-vaulted building, with arched dormer windows, central cupola, domed entrance and Art Nouveau tiling, not far from the railway bridge at the bottom of the High Street, was built as a Temperance Billiard Hall in 1908-10.

Temperance Billiard Halls Ltd was one of several companies established in the early twentieth century to build billiard halls *'to move billiards away from public houses and the vices of drink into an environment of teetotalism where both the working and middle class man could enjoy the game'*. This particular company was founded in Manchester in 1906, and soon spread its activities to London, where between 1909 and 1914 nine new halls were built, mostly in south-west London.

The company architect at the time was Norman Evans. The Clapham building, now well restored and maintained, is his best surviving work. Although there are other halls in Fulham, Lewisham and Wandsworth Road, they are much altered and neglected. His distinctive style incorporates Arts and Crafts and Art Nouveau features, and the dome, which is common to all Evans' buildings, defines the group identity.

The construction of the building is interesting as it is a very early example of the use of Ferro-concrete, a form of re-inforced concrete. This was first used in France at the end of the nineteenth century, and only slowly adopted in England. It was particularly useful to obtain the large unrestricted floor space required for a billiard hall. Ten reinforced concrete arches support the concrete shell of the barrel vault, providing an uninterrupted 650 square metres of floor space.

By the 1930s there were estimated to be up to 1500 billiard halls in London, but the vogue gradually passed and the Clapham Billiard Hall was put to various uses, mainly as storage, and was sadly neglected until Moxley Architects acquired the building in 1988. They undertook a major restoration of both the interior and exterior, reconstructing the wood and lead dome and restoring original tiles and glass. In addition they installed a mezzanine floor to make a more convenient office space, but this could be removed to reveal the original floor space. This is now a striking and unique landmark in Clapham High Street.

Former Temperance Billiard Hall,
No. 47 Clapham High Street

Board Schools

There were once several schools in the area of Clapham High Street. The only one to survive into the twenty-first century is Clapham Manor School in Belmont Road. Clapham Grammar School, mentioned above, closed before the end of the nineteenth century, but two more schools – Haselrigge and Aristotle Road – lasted for most of the twentieth century until they fell victim to the reduced demand for schools and increased demand for housing.

Just off the High Street at the end of St Luke's Avenue and Kenwyn Road is the former Haselrigge Primary School. This was Clapham's most flamboyant Board School, one of the many schools built in London as a result of the 1870 Education Act which required local School Boards to build and maintain schools out of the rates. It was built in 1885-86 to a design by T J Bailey, the architect of the School Board for London, in the Queen Anne revival style in red brick, with steeply pitched roofs and Dutch gables.

It is a particularly tall and large building, which makes a bold statement among the uniform terraces which surround it. The distinguished surgeon, Russell Brock, (1930–80) started his education here. The school closed in 1999, and the listed building was converted into flats.

In Aristotle Road further down the High Street towards Clapham North was Aristotle Road Secondary School. This was originally a girls' elementary school and later became a boys' school, at which the Clapham-born artist, Tom Phillips, taught Art, Music and English in the early 1960s after graduating from Oxford and while attending evening classes in art before becoming a full-time artist. The building was demolished after the school closed in the early 1990s, and a housing development, Aristotle Mews, was built on the site. All that remains of the school buildings is the former Schoolkeeper's Lodge, a pretty Arts and Crafts cottage built in the 1890s.

Opposite page: Former Haselrigge School

The Art Room at Aristotle Road Girls' School, 1908

Around Bromfelde Road

The map of 1849 shows no roads and very few buildings between Larkhall Lane and Clapham Road (then called Clapham Rise) east of Clapham Manor Street as far as Union Road. In the middle of the area was a large house, The Retreat, originally the home of the Hankey family. After they left Clapham for rural Surrey, it became a *'madhouse'* opened by Dr G M Burrows in 1832, who for most of his life *'devoted himself entirely to the treatment of insanity'*. One of the more distinguished inmates was William Buckland, Dean of Westminster Abbey,

who died there in 1856. Dr Burrows died in 1846 but The Retreat continued under new ownership until 1874 when it was demolished by George Hankey for the development of the Clapham Rise Estate.

The estate was laid out by local architect, E B I'Anson and built from 1875 onwards by several different local builders. The large well-built houses which line wide streets are most distinctive and unusual. In Gauden Road are terraces in fairly restrained Italianate style, while Sibella Road and Bromfelde Road have terraces of paired houses with two storeys at the

side rising to three storeys in the centre which makes them look rather like castles. In Chelsham Road are two very good detached double-fronted houses and a little lane which leads past the railed garden of St John's Church to the church itself and to Clapham Road.

Clapham's first picture palace, The Electric Vaudeville, once stood near the High Street end of Gauden Road. Fern Lodge, the impressive double fronted house with a Gothic arched front door, was built as a grammar school but has been a club for many years.

Clapham Road

One of the main routes out from the City of London to the country was Clapham Road, formerly called Clapham Rise. The street was once lined with large detached family houses, set back from the road with fields and orchards behind. Many were later turned into flats and joined into terraces, sometimes with Victorian features added, but there are still some original features visible and several houses have been well restored. The finest remaining house, now converted to flats, is No. 369, which has semi-circular bows and original wrought iron railings.

Opposite page: Bromfelde Road, 1977

No. 369 Clapham Road

There have been several notable residents in these grand houses, including the botanist, Nathaniel Bagshaw Ward (1791-1868), who introduced the glass case initially for growing plants in the smoky atmosphere of the Victorian house, but later used to transport plant specimens from the tropics without the need for watering them. He lived at No. 397; next door in a house now demolished lived the artist George Cattermole, who was a friend of Charles Dickens and illustrated many of his novels.

Until the early twenty-first century another of Clapham's many laundries, the Savoy Laundry, was on the north side of the road, near Union Road, with a delightful secluded garden. This has now been replaced by a large housing development.

Opposite No. 369 the Church of St John the Evangelist was built in 1840-42 in classical style, a very late use of this style for the Church of England and St John's was much criticised by the Gothicists. The church was considerably altered in the 1880s by the London Schools architect, T J Bailey. It is unusual in that the altar is now behind the central door, under the portico. In the late 1980s a screen was built which matches the internal galleries and is used to divide the church into two distinct spaces – a parish church and a church hall.

A little further to the west St Bede's Church was built in 1922-24 by Edward Maufe, architect of Guildford Cathedral, for the Royal Association for the Deaf and Dumb. The church was repaired after serious war damage, and is now in use as a Centre for Deaf People.

Larkhall Estate

Between Larkhall Lane and Wandsworth Road are two large estates, Larkhall and Springfield. In the early nineteenth century the area was owned by the Whidbourne family who built attractive detached villas along the two roads. When the leases expired in the early 1920s Sir Theodore Chambers, who then controlled the estate and was a strong advocate of the garden city principles, decided these principles should be applied in an inner city context. He formed a company to build well-planned homes in a landscaped environment for tenants on low incomes. The architects Louis de Soissons and G Grey Wornum were commissioned to design the estate, which served as a prototype for the neo-Georgian estates built by the London County Council over the next few years.

The five blocks of flats are built around landscaped courtyards. Most flats open onto balconies and many originally had direct access to roof gardens. Well in advance of their time, the flats had constant hot water, fitted kitchens and even washing machines. The development was opened in 1929 by Neville Chamberlain, then Minister of Health and later Prime Minister. The estate was modernised in the 1980s and is proudly maintained by residents.

To the east of Albion Avenue is the Springfield Estate. This land was sold by the Whidbourne family to the London County Council in 1936 and the estate built in the next few years along the same lines as the Larkhall Estate, but more austere and plain. In recent years attempts have been made to improve it by landscaping the grassed areas.

In Union Grove it is worth looking at the Police Station of 1907 and Christ Church, and its adjoining vicarage. The church was built in 1862 by Benjamin Ferrey, with some interior works by G E Street, the architect of the Law Courts in The Strand. Street was also the architect of the vicarage. Although difficult to see behind a high wall it is in Arts and Crafts style and looks as though it belongs in a country village, with its timber casement windows and clay tile hipped roof.

A courtyard in the Larkhall Estate

4 – Clapham Park

St Mary's Church

In Clapham Park Road St Mary's Church, or, to use its correct title, Our Lady of Victories, was built in 1849–51 by the architect William Wardell, a pupil of A W N Pugin. Wardell later emigrated to Australia and several churches and public buildings in Sydney and Melbourne are designed by him. The spire of St Mary's, which is a local landmark, is the only one remaining of the three church spires once known as the *'Three Sisters of Clapham'*. The two other spires belonging to the Methodist Church in Clapham High Street and the Congregational Church in Grafton Square were both destroyed by bombing in the Second World War.

The church was built on the grounds of part of a large house, once the home of Samuel Thornton and later of Lord Teignmouth, a member of the Clapham Sect. The house had been divided into two, and the occupant of the other half, Mr Soltau, was infuriated by the ringing of the church bells only feet from his windows. He obtained an injunction preventing the ringing of the bells during his lifetime. In the 1890s the old house was demolished, the church extended and the monastery built.

The Lady Chapel and a transept chapel as well as the adjoining Redemptorist monastery are by the local architect J F Bentley, whose son was responsible for later additions. The monastery, in red brick, has a Flemish look about it,

St Mary's Monastery and Church

51

and behind the high castellated wall along St Alphonsus Road is a large shady garden – all that remains of the garden of Samuel Thornton's mansion. At the end of the garden St Mary's Boys' School was built early in the twentieth century, but later it merged with the girls' school in Crescent Lane and the buildings are now used by Ace of Clubs as a day centre for the homeless.

In the churchyard is a war memorial by Sir Giles Gilbert Scott, erected in 1920. In 1868 the opera singer, Adelina Patti, who was living in Clapham Park at the time, married the Marquis de Caux at St Mary's Church.

William Bonney Estate

In the late nineteenth century Nelson's Row and White's Square were notorious slums, shown on Charles Booth's poverty map in the grade of *'very poor'*. In the early 1930s the local authority compulsorily purchased all the properties at the start of a major slum clearance programme in the area. In 1935 Harold Baily was appointed architect for the scheme which provided for 181 flats and six shops, and building started in 1938. Rents were to be 6s. 10d. (34p) per week for a one-bedroom flat and 8s. 10d. (44p) per week for a three-bedroom flat. However, before construction was completed, the war intervened and bombing destroyed many of the nearby houses in Park Crescent and along Clapham Park Road.

From 1948-50 the estate was extended with large blocks of red brick flats with concrete balconies and walkways. These are set around areas of grass and open play space, and there is a single storey nursery school with a double-bow glazed façade. The name of the estate commemorates William Bonney, the Mayor of Wandsworth during the Second World War.

One of the first Elim Pentecostal churches in this country opened in 1922 in Clapham Crescent. Two years later a youth branch, the Elim Crusaders, was started, and from here the youth movement spread throughout the British Isles. That building was destroyed by bombing in the Second World War, but was replaced by a new building on the same site.

Elim Church, Clapham Crescent

Park Hill and Northbourne Road

Park Hill was first laid out with suburban villas from 1830-50. Only a few of these survive, mostly now divided into flats. Park Hill House, which occupied a large site near the junction of Clapham Park Road, was the home of Charles Webb, father of the artist, Edward Webb, and grandfather of Sir Aston Webb, architect of the Victoria & Albert Museum. A later resident was the anthropologist, General Pitt Rivers, whose collection formed the basis of the Pitt Rivers Museum in Oxford. The land behind the house became a small industrial estate, as it still is, where the textile company, Courtaulds, first developed acetate fabrics.

St James's Church was built in 1957-58 to replace an earlier church destroyed by a bomb in 1940 when 300 people were in the shelter under the church – all emerged safely. The former church was an elaborate Gothic structure by the architect Lewis Vulliamy, in strong contrast to the present stark brick church designed by N F Cachemaille Day.

From 1946-66 two villas and their gardens near the church were the works and headquarters of the Allard Motor Company, whose showroom was in Clapham High Street. The villas were later converted to flats, and a new block of flats built in the garden, with access from Briarwood Road. The former connection is recalled by their name – Allard Gardens.

Northbourne Road was a speculative development of about 1860 by the builder, Henry Harris, who was particularly active in South Kensington. The attractive semi-detached houses in Northbourne Road have survived in good condition. Harris himself lived in West Road at Alver Bank, which has now been converted to an old peoples' home, and a sheltered housing block built behind.

Northbourne Road

Allard P1 (1949-52).
Allard's best-seller and the model in which
Sydney Allard won the 1952 Monte Carlo Rally

Cubitt's Clapham Park

In the late 1820s Thomas Cubitt, who had already developed a large area north of the river, around Belgravia and Pimlico, leased about 200 acres of farmland in Clapham on which he started to lay out the series of wide avenues of Clapham Park. He envisaged the area as a garden suburb of London, but it was never as successful as he had hoped, largely because the simultaneous expansion of the railways meant that commuters could conveniently travel further out to the country.

Cubitt built some substantial detached villas himself and sold other sites. Today only a very few of the original villas, which once lined Kings Avenue, Poynders Road and Atkins Road, still survive. Those which do have been much altered over the years, and demolished villas have been replaced by an eclectic mix of houses and blocks of flats.

In the nineteenth century several well-known people chose these detached villas with good gardens as their homes. General Sir William Napier, historian and prolific writer, lived at a house which he named Scinde House, commemorating his brother's conquest of the Indian province with that name. Later the music hall star Vesta Victoria lived in the house which she renamed Victoria House. This Cubitt house now converted to flats, can still be seen in Kings Avenue (No. 84).

Other notable residents of Clapham Park included the Mappin brothers, cutlers from Sheffield, who founded Mappin & Webb, jewellers of Regent Street and the artist, Douglas Stannus Grey.

Thomas Cubitt.
Statue in Denbigh
Street, Pimlico
by William Fawke, 1995

Thomas Cubitt's own house, Lincoln House, stood in extensive grounds on the western edge of Clapham Park. The house was demolished in 1905 to make way for Rodenhurst Road, but one relic remains in Clarence Avenue – Clifton Lodge, which was probably built for his gardener, John Clifton. It is a charming cottage with low-pitched gables and the square chimney pots seen on many of Cubitt's buildings.

Sadly it is under threat in 2006 for the extension of the nearby estate.

Thomas Cubitt's house was reached by a 100 metre tree-lined drive from the main entrance on Poynders Road. In addition to the usual reception room, library and billiard room the house had 14 bedrooms, a servants' wing, a stable yard for four carriages and horses, a cowhouse, aviary, vinery, walled fruit and kitchen gardens, lawns, flowerbeds and secluded walks among the trees and shrubberies. The house was named Lincoln House by a later owner, Isaac Seligman, who was a great admirer of the American President.

Lincoln House, home of Thomas Cubitt.
Lithograph by an unknown artist, around 1860

Clifton Lodge, the sole surviving building by Cubitt in the grounds of Lincoln House. This can now be seen in Clarence Avenue.

Opposite page: Victoria House,
No. 84 Kings Avenue

1930s houses in Clarence Avenue

There were once several large detached houses with gardens in Clarence Avenue, but these were demolished after war damage and much of the road was redeveloped in the 1950s and 1960s. First Clapham Park Estate spread along Clarence Avenue from the South Circular Road and then the tower blocks, set in landscaped grounds and with underground parking, were built near to Park Hill. In the 1930s a few semi-detached houses just off Kings Avenue had been built. These are roughcast and most retain their metal casement windows, typical of the period.

Among the notable residents of the early twentieth century houses of Rodenhurst Road were Arthur Henderson (1863-1935) the first Labour MP to become a member (in 1915) of Lloyd George's wartime coalition cabinet and William Bonney, Mayor of Wandsworth during the Second World War.

Arthur Henderson and his family at home, about 1920

Clapham Park Estate

Clapham Park Estate was originally an area of about 15 acres on either side of Atkins Road at the junction with New Park Road.

The development started in 1930 with 20 five- and six-storey blocks of flats, built of red brick in neo-Georgian style, with pitched tiled roofs, bay windows and some concrete balconies. They were designed for the London County Council by their architect, G Topham Forrest, and named after members of the first School Board for London, one of whom, Sir Thomas Tilson, lived in Atkins Road.

The estate was first extended in 1953 with two-storey houses, flats and maison-ettes with frontages on Kings Avenue. Then in 1955 Clapham Park West, on the west side of Kings Avenue, was started. Five and six-storey blocks were built to fill the area bounded by Kings Avenue, Poynders Road and Clarence Avenue. The style was influenced by New Town architecture, with balcony access flats and a horizontal emphasis. Playgrounds, a library, nursery and primary school were included in the scheme.

Over the years the housing became neglected and run-down and in 2000 the Clapham Park Project, one of the largest housing regeneration schemes in London, was awarded £56 million under the New Deal for Communities programme. Ownership of the estate was transferred from Lambeth Council to Clapham Park Homes in 2006. About 50% of properties are to be refurbished, and the rest demolished and replaced by new housing. The scheme also includes a new health centre, community and sports facilities, new shops as well as another primary school, a new bus facility and landscaped parks and courtyards. The eastern (original) part of Clapham Park Estate will be refurbished and Clapham Park West will be largely replaced.

Clapham Park Estate in the snow. Winter 2003. Photograph by Andrew Walker

Abbeville Road

The large Georgian houses which lined Clapham Common South Side had grounds which extended back to reach those of the houses around Clarence Road, now called Clarence Avenue. It was not until 1865 that the first houses at the Common end of Elms Road were built, and a few years later the houses at the junction of Cavendish Road and Abbeville Road followed.

Gradually over the next fifty years all the large houses were demolished and their grounds sold for the development of the terraced houses which now line the streets around Abbeville Road. While the first houses in Abbeville Road itself were large family homes, the centre of the street became then, as it is now, mainly shops. Early twentieth century pictures show a variety of shops including a large dairy from which milk was delivered by hand-pushed carts, a bakery and a florist. By the early twenty-first century the street had become well-known for its restaurants

and bars, as well as a welcome selection of small shops.

On the corner of Crescent Lane two trade union headquarters were built in the 1930s. The Builders, the home of the building trades' union, is still in use by the merged union, but the former Post Office Workers' Union left Clapham when it merged, and that building is now the offices of the Metropolitan Housing Trust.

In Narbonne Avenue the Church of the Holy Spirit was built in 1912-13 as a memorial to Canon Charles Philip Greene, Rector of Clapham, who died in 1908. From the outside it is a rather forbidding-looking brown brick Gothic building, but the lofty interior is impressive with nave and chancel of the same height and whitewashed vaulted ceiling.

The street names in this area, Abbeville, Narbonne, Bonneville, Trouville, might be supposed to indicate some historic link with the French. Disappointingly, they all result from negotiations between the developers and the Metropolitan Board of Works, which from 1856 had a rigid requirement that new street names must not duplicate any already existing in London.

Headquarters of the Union of Post Office Workers, Crescent Lane. Drawing by an unknown artist, 1937

Milk delivery carts lined up outside Welford's Dairy, No. 53 Abbeville Road, around 1907

Opposite page: Abbeville Road

La Retraite

La Retraite convent school was started by a group of nuns from Angers in France, who came to England in 1880. They eventually settled in Clapham Park, purchasing Oaklands in Atkins Road. As the school flourished over the years the nuns bought three more adjoining houses, The Oaks, Springfield and Burlington House. These four houses, originally built in 1857–62, were linked together but in 1937 The Oaks was demolished and replaced by a new chapel and dining room.

During the Second World War the school was evacuated to two large rambling houses in Hampshire. After the war La Retraite became a grammar school, and in 1957 St Bernadette's Primary School was added. In 1977 new buildings were added when La Retraite became comprehensive, and in 1990 the convent and school were separated.

Springfield, the house which was added to La Retraite in 1904, had been the home of the music hall artist, Dan Leno, – *'the funniest man on earth'*. He became very rich and famous and his lavishly decorated house had three acres of land and stabling behind. Dan Leno was so popular that huge crowds lined the three-mile route of his funeral procession. A hearse drawn by six horses was followed by a number of mourning coaches, three open landaus filled with wreaths and floral tributes, and over 60 private carriages.

The crowd at the cemetery was so great that it broke down the entrance gate, according to a report in *The Clapham Observer*. His memorial is engraved *'Here sleeps the King of Laughter Makers'*.

Dan Leno in Mother Goose. 1902

La Retraite Roman Catholic Girls' School, Atkins Road

5 – Clapham Common South Side

Clapham Cross

The underground first came to Clapham in 1900 when the City & South London Line, which at that time terminated at Stockwell, was extended to Clapham Common. This remained the end of the line until 1926 when a further seven stations were opened to continue the line as far as Morden. The original Clapham Common station was on the corner of Clapham Park Road and Clapham High Street, where hoardings now obscure the entrance to the deep shelter built on the site in 1940-42, at the same time as the one at Clapham South (See page 72).

The entrance to Clapham Common station was moved to its present location in 1924 when the station was completely remodelled by the architect Charles Holden. Holden had been chosen, on the recommendation of the legendary Frank Pick, most famous as the designer of the schematic map of London Underground, to reconstruct the stations on the existing City & South London Line and to design the new ones for the extension to Morden. In South London, the stations at Oval, Kennington and Clapham North, as well as Clapham Common, were remodelled, the booking halls and platforms being given standard black and white tiling. The other stations had new cream slab facades, but at Clapham Common the distinctive Portland stone rotunda with a

The original entrance to Clapham Common Underground Station on the corner of Clapham Park Road and Clapham High Street, around 1910

glass dome is all that can be seen of the station above ground. Clapham Common and Clapham North are the only two stations on the former City & South London Line (now the Northern Line) which still have central island platforms.

The Clock Tower, which was unveiled with great ceremony in 1906, was the gift of Alexander Glegg, the Mayor of Wandsworth at the time (the whole of Clapham was then in the Borough of Wandsworth). It was originally in a slightly different position on the island site and had to be moved to accommodate the new station entrances.

This area has always been the transport hub of Clapham. In the eighteenth century there was a coaching inn on the site of The Plough Inn, now SW4 Bar. It later became a departure point for horse drawn trams and omnibuses. One mid-nineteenth century writer records that the fare by omnibus from The Plough to town was sixpence (2.5p), but on the fast four-horse coach which ran from Balham it was one shilling (5p). The stables were behind The Plough, which was the tram terminus until the advent of the electric tram. In the early twentieth century tramlines were laid along South Side and in 1903 the Prince and Princess of Wales (later George V and Queen Mary) travelled in the first electric tram from Tooting to Clapham. In the 1920s the appearance of The Plough Inn was transformed when it was given a new frontage in mock-Tudor style.

The Alexandra

The Alexandra

The Alexandra and the buildings on either side were built in 1863 as a hotel. The architect was Edward I'Anson.

The Alexandra is an attractive building, typical of the period, with its patterns in coloured brickwork, fishtail slates and Gothic style pointed arched windows. Many original details have survived, including the elaborate ironwork on the domed roof and the window boxes. Sadly all the original interior fittings have long since been lost in various alterations.

In 1876 the hotel closed, the central section was converted to a public house and the flanking properties sold for separate use. Early photographs show the building without the dome, though it was added very early, and its purpose has never been established. For many years the first floor dining room was considered the best eating place in Clapham.

A little further along South Side the present Peoples' Republic bar has an interesting history. It was originally built as a Baptist Chapel in 1777. When the chapel became too small for the congregation a new church was built in Grafton Square and this building became a Post Office in 1886.

By 1960 the Post Office had closed and the building was converted to a restaurant. After further alterations in the 1970s it became a Wimpy Bar and then changed ownership several times until the present bar opened in 2005. For many years a plaque survived in an internal passageway recording that this had been a Baptist Chapel.

Crescent Grove

Two pairs of substantial stuccoed houses mark the narrow entrance to this private estate, built in 1825-27 by Francis Child as a family investment. One side is a crescent of terraced houses (originally called The Crescent) and the other is a series of semi-detached houses linked by coach houses (originally called The Grove). The houses were conveyed to various members of the Child family by Francis Child, and several residents have deeds showing when the houses were first sold out of the family.

Crescent Grove Estate is still privately owned and the residents are responsible for maintaining the roads and gardens, although *'lighting and watching'* which were also once included, have now been taken over by the local authority. The architect of the houses is unknown. They have been attributed to Thomas Cubitt who took a lease of a large area of Clapham in 1825, but there is no evidence to support this.

The houses have much interesting architectural detail, especially the iron-work. Some houses have original boot-scrapers, one still has an original dog railing to keep stray dogs off the doorstep, and the continuous balcony at first floor level of the crescent survives in good condition.

The railings round the basement areas have a unique crescent motif. Similar railings once enclosed the centre garden, but, like so many railings in London squares, they were removed during the Second World War when metal was being collected to help the war effort. Elaborate iron gates probably once marked the entrance from South Side.

Crescent Grove has had several well-known residents, including the Revd. Charles Pritchard, founder and head-master of Clapham Grammar School, the engineer James Wimshurst who built *'electric lighting machinery'* and the palaeontologist and *'discoverer of dinosaurs'*, Gideon Mantell. Mantell, a doctor by training, who became obsessed with collecting to the detriment of his medical practice, moved to Clapham from Brighton in 1838 when financial problems forced him to sell his collection. He lived in the house at the entrance to Crescent Grove, now called Denmark Lodge.

Gideon Mantell.
Engraving after a painting by J J Masquerier, 1837

Over page: Crescent Grove

Notre Dame Estate

Robert Thornton, the first member of the Hull merchant family to come to Clapham in about 1740, lived in a grand house on South Side. His son, John, and grandson, also Robert, lived in the next house, which, according to the sale details of the house in 1810, had extensive *'pleasure grounds'* including a lake and *'an extremely elegant and costly Greenhouse built of Portland Stone which is frequently used in the Summer as a Drawing Room'*. This building, now known as The Orangery, still survives in poor condition, rather incongruously surrounded by the blocks of flats of the Notre Dame Estate.

Robert Thornton junior entertained lavishly – Queen Charlotte and the Princesses Augusta and Elizabeth and the Prime Minister, William Pitt, dined with him in Clapham. But he also invested unwisely, with the result he went bankrupt and fled to America. In 1851 the two houses and grounds were bought by the Belgian sisters of Notre Dame, who linked the houses and established a convent school there. At the start of the Second World War the school was evacuated to the country, and the buildings were used by the Free French Forces during the war.

After a period of use as temporary housing after the war the houses were demolished to make way for the Notre Dame Estate, built by Wandsworth Council from 1947-52. The lake was filled in, and the gardens, which had been used by the convent school as playing fields, were covered with housing. The small terraces away from South Side were built first and the 8-storey blocks facing the Common were the last phase. These included novel features at the time – rooftop clothes drying areas and basement workshops, which later became garages. In 1952 the architect of the estate, C H James, won a Ministry of Housing and Local Government award for his design.

The Orangery, 1977

The Orangery in the grounds of the Notre Dame Convent School, around 1910

Henry Thornton School and its Successors

South Side was once lined with splendid houses. Where Lambeth College now stands were South Lodge, at one time the home of Frederick Gorringe who founded a famous store in Victoria, and Stowey House, which was once Clapham Rectory and later the home of the Strachey family where Lytton Strachey, author of *Eminent Victorians*, was born.

In 1914 the London County Council acquired both properties, which were used as an open-air school until 1929, when they became part of Henry Thornton Boys' Secondary School. The school had been founded in 1894 in Battersea and after several moves it came to Clapham, adopting the name appropriate to the area. The main classrooms were in a new block, built in the grounds behind the two houses, with an entrance from Elms Road.

The school flourished and a major redevelopment took place from 1966-69, which coincided with the change to comprehensive education. Both South Lodge and Stowey House were demolished and new buildings facing South Side were constructed. The design by architects Farmer & Dark included a swimming pool, theatre, classrooms and an administrative block as well as a football pitch within a hangar-like building. At the time the number of pupils increased from 450 to about 1500.

By 1987 the school roll had dropped, the buildings were neglected and Henry Thornton School merged with Hydeburn School on the latter's Balham site. In 1993 Lambeth College, one of the largest further education colleges in London opened in the refurbished South Side buildings. Meanwhile the 1929 building was used by Lambeth Council for adult education classes until it was demolished to make way for a new secondary school, Lambeth Academy, which opened in 2004.

In 2006 Lambeth College is planning further changes including part demolition and rebuilding of the South Side elevation to accommodate a proposed Sixth Form Centre.

Opposite page: Henry Thornton School, now Lambeth College, 1977

Henry Thornton School, 1939

The Windmill

In 1631 Dr Henry Atkins, Physician in Ordinary to King James I, leased to Richard Jarman the *'Wynd Mill, dwelling house and a little plott of ground about the sayd house now severed from the common'* for the sum of £8 a year. Thirty years later the rent was only £3 a year, which suggests the windmill may have been falling into disrepair, and it probably disappeared soon afterwards. The Windmill Inn, which is thought to occupy roughly the same site, is first mentioned in the early eighteenth century.

The core of the present building dates from the end of the eighteenth century, although it has been altered and added to at various times. Just behind the inn was Denny's dairy farm which later moved to Clapham Manor Street.

There was also a substantial house, called The White House, which was the home of the Young family for many years. A member of this same family, Charles Allen Young, was one of the founders of Young's Brewery in Wandsworth in 1831. It is a nice coincidence that for over 100 years The Windmill was owned by Young's Brewery. The White House was demolished in the 1890s and the pond in front of it filled in, when the red brick houses of Windmill Drive were built.

The Windmill was a popular coaching inn and is clearly identifiable in the background of a painting of about 1850, *The Return from the Derby*, by J F Herring. The painting shows the crowds which gathered to watch coaches passing through Clapham on the way to Epsom on Derby Day. The Windmill on the Common, as it is now called, is a hotel as well as a busy pub, and still an important landmark on South Side.

The Windmill on the Common

Eagle House

Almost opposite The Windmill, straddling what is now Narbonne Avenue, was Eagle House, built in 1773 by Benjamin Bond. From 1789 to 1800 it was the home of William Smith, MP, grandfather of Florence Nightingale and a friend of William Wilberforce, and a colleague in his campaign against the slave trade. A later resident of the house was William Edgar, co-founder of the department store, Swan & Edgar, who died there in 1869. His wife lived at Eagle House for a further 20 years.

The remains of Eagle House, Narbonne Avenue when in use as a chapel, 1966

The house had extensive grounds, which were described in great detail in an account of 1849. There was a conservatory 11m long by 6m wide, other glass-houses, a mushroom house, seed room and a hot-house for pineapples and French beans, strawberry beds and a vinery. On a walk round the estate one passed *'a cornshed of neat ornamental character, a farmyard, clean and tidy, a pretty cottage, an ornamental piece of water spanned by a bridge, a summer-house, then a hermitage, furnished with a tenant, a facsimile of that extinct race, with a grove of chestnuts connected with a grove of elms beyond, clothed with undergrowth of laurels, rhododendrons, and other evergreens, and to the house by a grove of Scotch pines'.*

The house was demolished in about 1891 and the entire estate covered by the houses of the streets stretching back to Abbeville Road. One small wing, which may once have been a billiard room on the south side of the house, survived. This was in use as a chapel in the 1960s and then fell into disrepair until it was rescued in 1989 by a local structural engineer, Sinclair Johnston, who refurbished the building as his office. The arcaded façade and Tuscan columns can still be seen a short way down Narbonne Avenue.

Rear view of Eagle House. Watercolour by Edward Hull, 1868

Deep Shelters

The ugly structure on the Common almost opposite the entrance to Clapham South Underground Station is the ventilation shaft and entrance to one of the deep shelters built in 1940-42 below the Northern Line. The shelters are now listed buildings. They were intended as wartime air raid shelters, but the sites were linked to existing underground stations so that they could be taken over after the war for the possible construction of an express underground railway. In fact, the building of the shelters made slow progress because by the time the first one was completed in 1942 the London blitz was over. The completed shelters were used only briefly as shelters in 1944-45 during the V1 and V2 rocket attacks.

There were two entrances to each shelter, and these can still be found at all three Clapham stations. Each shelter comprised two parallel tubes about 5 metres in diameter and 425 metres long, and was fully equipped with bunks, kitchens and sanitation. The express railway did not materialise and all the shelters have now been rented to private companies and are in use for archive document storage.

The shelters have, however, had other uses since the end of the Second World War. In 1948 West Indian immigrants arriving on *SS Empire Windrush*, who had no contacts in this country, were accommodated temporarily in the deep shelter at Clapham South. Many immigrants found jobs and homes locally, thus forming the basis of the West Indian community in South London.

The deep shelters, near Clapham South

Cavendish House

Cavendish House stood in extensive grounds, covering a large area south of Cavendish Road, then called Dragmire (or Dragmore) Lane, as far as Poynders Road. The house took its name from the eccentric scientist Henry Cavendish, who lived there from 1782 to 1810. Cavendish used the upper rooms of his house as an observatory, the drawing room as a laboratory, and had a forge in an adjoining room. He rarely had visitors, except for an occasional scientist visiting his extensive library, and was often to be seen walking down the middle of the road after dark in unusual and old-fashioned clothing. He had a particular dread of women, and is said to have communicated with his housekeeper by written notes.

Because of the experiments he conducted concerning gravity Cavendish became known as *'the man who weighed the world'*.

An earlier owner, and possibly the builder of the house, was Henton Brown whose activities at the Mount Pond are described in Chapter 6.

Thomas Cubitt lived at Cavendish House before his own house in Clapham Park was completed. A later occupant was Henry Sandford Bicknell, son-in-law of the artist, David Roberts. Bicknell had inherited his father's important art collection to which he added considerably – in particular many pictures by David Roberts. On Bicknell's death in 1880 the art collection was sold at Christies and the property was put up for auction. The catalogue described a house with *'a handsome Library, Billiard-room, large Conservatory and 17 bedrooms…'* as well as *'Pleasure Grounds enriched with stately Timber of Cedar, Oak, Beech, Fir and Cypress laid out with a Terrace Walk, Lake and Summer Houses…kitchen garden.., orchard house, aloe house and two vineries'*.

Within 25 years all this was to disappear, when the estate was sold for development and the whole area was covered with terraced houses.

Interior of Cavendish House, around 1870

The Former South London Hospital

The large red brick building almost opposite Clapham South Underground Station was part of the South London Hospital for Women from 1935 to 1984. The hospital was originally opened in 1916 in a building, now demolished, which stood slightly further south. The founder was Dr Maud Chadburn, a pioneering surgeon and a colleague of Elizabeth Garrett Anderson. Dr Chadburn was determined to establish a hospital for women in south London along the same lines as the one started some years earlier in north London by Elizabeth Garrett Anderson. She eventually succeeded, despite formidable opposition from her, mainly male, colleagues.

In 1935 the hospital increased considerably in size. A new front block was designed in neo-Georgian style by the architect Sir Edwin Cooper. The hospital flourished and was always very popular. The Cooper building was to have been extended, but the Second World War prevented that. In the early 1980s St George's Health Trust, under whose control the hospital then was, proposed closing the South London Hospital and transferring the services to St George's Hospital at Tooting.

The proposal resulted in an unprecedented level of opposition, which developed

The Cooper building adapted and extended by Tesco

into a national campaign. Many former patients were involved. One even wrote to the Queen and presented a petition with 55,000 signatures to the Prime Minister in Downing Street. Because banners were not allowed she knitted herself a white cardigan with *'Save South London Hospital'* on the back in navy blue. But this was all to no avail, the battle was lost and the hospital finally closed in 1984. It then emerged that the founders of the hospital had made provision in the event of closure, which resulted in a dispute over ownership of the land. It was ten years later before an agreement was reached that the site be sold and the proceeds divided between the regional health authority and London University. The capital acquired by the University was invested and the income is used to fund five Chadburn lectureships, one at each of the University's five medical schools. On part of the land at the back of the site Minnie Kidd Nursing Home for the frail elderly was built.

Objections and dispute about the planning application for a major supermarket in this position followed, and it was another ten years before Tesco were granted permission for a supermarket on the condition that the original Cooper building was retained. The supermarket finally opened in 2005, the upper part was converted to flats, with car parking and a new block of flats behind.

South London Hospital, the Outpatients Department, 1977

6 – Clapham Common

Battersea Woods

Battersea Woods is the part of the Common which most closely resembles its original appearance. Like all commons, Clapham Common was a relic of medieval agriculture, waste land that could not profitably be used for crops. Archaeologists have found prehistoric remains, and there were attempts at farming in the thirteenth century; but better land lay to the north. The Common itself was rough and poorly drained, full of ditches and often waterlogged. But it had its uses, for grazing of cattle and other livestock; pigs could root for nuts in the woods, and the villagers could gather brushwood and furze for their ovens.

The transformation to the park-like scene we see today began in the mid-eighteenth century. *'Thirty years ago the Common was little better than a morass,'* wrote Daniel Lysons in 1792. He recorded the first improvements, led by Christopher Baldwin, who had a house on West Side and was a local magistrate. He and other residents subscribed money, and gradually the small scrubby trees were replaced by new planting and the rough ground was levelled and drained.

While Battersea Woods may recall the ancient Common, especially in wet winter periods, none of its trees are old. The hawthorns date in part from the Edwardian period and in part from the 1930s, when the London County Council ran relief schemes for the unemployed, who were paid to plant the trees at the rate of a shilling (5p) per tree.

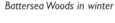
Battersea Woods in winter

Joseph Powell

Around 1820 the topographical artist Joseph Powell made a number of sketches and engravings of the Common, giving us the first insights into how it looked. Many of the pictures show the Common as a place of work; horses being watered, carts drawing fresh water from the springs, washing hung out to dry. Others show new planting and people strolling for pleasure.

In the opening years of the nineteenth century the young Tom Macaulay, the future historian, made the Common his playground. His nephew and biographer described '*that delightful wilderness of gorse bushes, and poplar groves, and gravel pits, and ponds great and small*'. There was a slight ridge, intersected by ditches, towards the west of the Common, and the young Macaulay called this the Alps – not to be confused with the raised area to the north of the all-weather pitches now nicknamed the Alps, the creation of a Common Superintendent in the 1980s.

The picture here shows sheep, donkeys and cattle. The view is taken from about the site of the present bandstand, looking east with rough ground in front of the Mount Pond (to the right). On the left is a group of trees known as the Nine Elms, planted around 1780, the last of which survived until 1970. The Common had many fine elms, but all were devastated by Dutch Elm Disease in the 1980s.

'View from the Nine Elms on Clapham Common, looking SE'.
Lithograph by Joseph Powell, 1825

Parish Boundaries

At several points on the Common there are cast iron posts, inscribed either Battersea or Clapham. Two easily found are in the vicinity of the bandstand and just by the path which leads from Battersea Woods towards the north-east side of the Common.

In the seventeenth and eighteenth centuries the boundary was disputed, the manor and parish of Clapham claiming the whole of the Common. Trouble broke out in 1716, when the people of Battersea, claiming that Clapham people were monopolising the grazing, dug a ditch and bank

A boundary marker on Clapham Common

across the Common. Clapham filled in the ditch and demolished the bank. In 1718 and 1719 representatives of the two manors went to law. The courts do not seem to have given a ruling that settled the matter, but the witness statements survived in the public records, and give a fascinating picture of life in Clapham in those times.

In the nineteenth century the boundaries were still in dispute. A map of the parish of Clapham made in 1849 shows the parish boundary running along West Side. When the two parishes conducted the ceremony of Beating of the Bounds there were sometimes scuffles, and letters passed between the lords of the two manors and the churches. In 1859 the Clapham procession went along West Side, and through the front garden of Field Marshal Sir George Pollock, hero of the Afghan Wars. He complained: '*I don't know of whom all the Mob consisted, but I hear that the Rector of Clapham was there, also one of his Curates*'. It did not happen again, and a few years later the marker posts were put up.

The boundaries of the parishes thus marked are now the boundaries of the Boroughs of Lambeth and Wandsworth, though since 1971, when the Greater London Council gave up its open spaces, Lambeth has owned the whole of the Common.

The Ponds

There are four ponds on the Common, but there were once many more: early nineteenth century maps show eleven. Some were natural, but many more were created by digging for gravel for making the improved main roads of the eighteenth century. That is the likely origin of the Mount Pond, though the raised island in the middle was made in the 1740s by a wealthy banker, Henton Brown. He built a bridge and summerhouse, and moored his boat on the pond, behaving as if it was his private property. The other inhabitants subsequently put a stop to that, insisting that Brown paid a hefty rent; and they became very vigilant to prevent further attempts to appropriate bits of the Common. As well as planting trees and levelling the rough ground, they prevented further gravel digging and landscaped the sides of the ponds.

In the nineteenth century a further step was taken; a group of residents took a lease of the Common from the lords of the two manors, so that they could manage the Common as a public open space. Under their control many of the ponds were filled in.

In the twentieth century the Mount Pond has been used for boating, as was the Eagle Pond near The Windmill pub, and boys used to swim in it (girls were not allowed). In recent years both the Mount and Eagle Ponds have been used for fishing, but a part of each is reserved for wild life, and reed beds have improved the ecology.

Mount Pond, Clapham Common. Watercolour by Edward Hull, 1869

Eagle Pond

78

Benjamin Franklin

The Mount Pond was the probable scene of a scientific experiment by the American philosopher and statesman Benjamin Franklin. On two sea voyages he had noticed that greasy water thrown overboard by the cooks had the effect of smoothing the waves; fishermen and divers, he discovered, knew the advantages of pouring oil on troubled waters. In the early 1770s he resolved to try an experiment. He was staying with his friends the Baldwins at their house on West Side, and his London banker was Henton Brown, who lived on South Side. The experiment took place on a pond somewhere between their houses, and the generally accepted view is that this was the Mount Pond.

Franklin chose a day when the surface of the pond was rough with wind, and poured on it a teaspoonful of oil. He was amazed to find not just the expected result that the oil calmed the waters, but also that the oil spread in a thin film over the whole pond. He repeated the experiment on other ponds and lakes and on the sea at Spithead, developing a scientific theory based on the mutual repulsion of oil and water. Later scientists picked up the significance of Franklin's work for the study of surface tension and of particle size.

Benjamin Franklin. Painting by Jean-Baptiste Greuze, 1777

Speakers' Corner

To the south of the Mount Pond is an area with a hard surface used for circuses and fun fairs, and often known as the Ashes. The end nearest Windmill Drive was designated as a Speakers' Corner.

Public speaking on Clapham Common can be traced to at least the mid-nineteenth century, though it took place on a site nearer the centre of the Common, moving here when the bandstand was built in 1890. Among the speakers was the radical politician John Burns, who was arrested for illegal speaking in contravention of the by-laws in 1878.

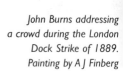

John Burns addressing a crowd during the London Dock Strike of 1889. Painting by A J Finberg

Among the spectators impressed by the incident was the lady who later became his wife.

John Burns made his name nationally as the leader of the London dockers' strike in 1889. In 1892 he became the MP for Battersea South as an independent labour candidate, and when the Labour Party was formed he stayed outside it.

In 1905 he entered the Liberal Government's Cabinet, the first working man to serve there. He resigned in 1914, disillusioned by the outbreak of the First World War. A blue plaque marks his house on North Side, where he lived until his death in 1943.

Speakers' Corner became a popular place for Sunday afternoon speakers,

second only to Hyde Park. George Bernard Shaw was among the politicians who spoke there, and religious speakers and secularists competed for attention. In his novel *The End of the Affair*, set in Clapham around the Second World War, Graham Greene included scenes with a faith healer.

Public speaking continued after the War, but gradually declined and ceased.

Sport

The tennis courts and bowling green on West Side are part of a long tradition of sport, formal or informal, on the Common. In the seventeenth century there was archery, horse riding and even an early mention of cricket. Later, there were boxing matches; and football, organised or otherwise, has been played for centuries. Organised football with clear rules is a product of the mid-nineteenth century, and one of the earlier members of the Football Association was Clapham Rovers. They played on the Common in the early 1870s, but moved to Wandsworth Common, which was their base in 1880, the year they won the FA Cup. A golf club was founded in 1873, and from 1905 until 1939 play was allowed on a nine-hole course on the Common from about 6.15 to 9.00 am (it was thought too hazardous any later). Bowls and tennis were also well established by the early twentieth century.

Returning to the main part of the Common, alongside The Avenue, we find a double line of trees with a wide track between them, a former horse ride. Riding was once a popular pastime. According to the witnesses in the eighteenth century lawsuits, the ground had been cleared between The Windmill and the west side of the Common to allow racing. When the Metropolitan Board of Works bought the Common in 1877 (so preserving it for ever in public ownership) one of its first landscaping works was to lay out this ride.

Just off Rookery Road there are netball courts built by the London County Council around 1950 in an area which had been occupied by prefabs in the Second World War. Netball contests took place here, though now the courts are more usually used for informal basketball. Much of the open green space is laid out as sports pitches, but the whole space has long been used for informal recreation. The Common is windy, and kite flying has a long history. Otherwise the use of the Common reflects changing practices. There used to be regular chess games by the bandstand café, but that has died out. Model boating on the Long Pond goes back to the 1870s, but is in danger of dying out. Throwing frisbees, jogging and skateboarding are popular now, and no doubt other activities will come along in the future.

The tennis courts and bowling green, Clapham Common West Side

The World Wars

Both the World Wars of the twentieth century had a major impact on the Common. In both wars large parts of the Common were turned to use as allotments, and in the First World War an area near the west end of North Side was used for training in digging of trenches.

In the Second World War air-raid shelters were built round the edges of the Common, mostly along West Side. Although the steps down to the shelters were filled in after the War, the asphalted tops remain to this day. In the part of the Common lying between the Long Pond and the bandstand there was a large camp with batteries of anti-aircraft guns, the soldiers being housed in temporary huts. Prefabs for emergency housing of families who had lost their homes in the bombing were built along Long Road and South Side, remaining there until the 1950s.

Aerial photos taken by archaeologists have identified the sites where all this activity took place, but no trace is now visible on the ground.

Holy Trinity Church with allotments on the Common during the Second World War. Watercolour by S R Badmin, 1940

Anti-aircraft guns on Clapham Common, around 1940

The Drinking Fountain

The bronze figures on the drinking fountain are the work of a German sculptor, August von Kreling, cast in 1884, and depict a woman giving water to a beggar. The fountain originally stood in the City of London; it was erected by the United Kingdom Temperance and General Provident Society, and their badge and the arms of the City are on either side of the plinth. It stood outside their offices on the northern approach to London Bridge, and it is said that its weight had begun to crack the bridge approach. It was removed here in 1895.

Close to it is a large black poplar. This replaced a similar large tree which was known as Captain Cook's tree. In fact the great explorer never lived in Clapham (see Chapter 3). His son, another Captain James Cook, did plant some trees on the Common.

The nearby paddling pool was once the Cock Pond, so called after the pub which is now the Frog and Forget-me-not, and one of the many ponds on the Common. It was concreted in 1936 and has remained a popular children's paddling pool.

The Temperance Fountain

The paddling pool, 2003

The Horse Show

From 1954 to 1985 the Common was used for one of London's most popular August Bank Holiday events, the County of London (later Greater London) Horse Show. It started as a modest gymkhana, but by the 1960s grew to attract international show-jumpers of Olympic standard, including Princess Anne. There were carriage driving displays and a regular attraction was the parade of the great horses from Young's and other breweries. There were military displays and historical re-enactments. When the London County Council, which had started the show, was replaced by the Greater London Council, the GLC continued it; it lapsed when the GLC handed over its parks to the boroughs.

The Horse Show was the largest and most popular of the events on the Common in the decades after the Second World War. The LCC also provided open-air ballet, theatre in a tent and boxing.

In the 1990s the Common started to be used for big events put on not by Councils but by outside promoters. Some caused considerable disruption by their size or noise, and the extent to which it is appropriate to use an urban open space for large events has been a matter of controversy.

The Greater London Horse Show, 1964

The Bandstand

Built in 1890, the Bandstand is the oldest and largest surviving in Greater London, and one of the largest ever built in England. In the summer of 1888 the Metropolitan Police Band gave regular outdoor concerts on Wednesday afternoons; local shops closed on these afternoons to allow assistants to *'enjoy rest and relaxation'* by hearing the music. These were so popular that local residents successfully petitioned the London County Council to provide a bandstand.

At that time the LCC had just acquired two bandstands, salvaged from the gardens of the Royal Horticultural Society in South Kensington, which had recently closed. These bandstands had been built by Francis Fowke for the gardens when they opened in 1861. Fowke's bandstands were re-erected in Southwark Park and Peckham Rye, and the contractor who was shifting them suggested that a copy might be made for Clapham Common. The LCC's architect Thomas Blashill took up the idea, and designed a replica, with some modifications to stay within a £600 budget.

The next twenty years were a great period for band concerts. Professional bands were coming in, as well as the traditional police and military bands. By 1905 the Head of LCC parks could write that Clapham was *'one of the most frequented of all the commons... on Saturday afternoons especially it is teeming with London toilers'.* Use of the bandstand continued into the

years after the Second World War. But by the 1960s and 70s traditional cast iron bandstands were thought old fashioned, and by the late 1980s use of the bandstand had virtually ceased. The bandstand became derelict, in 1997 it was put on English Heritage's Buildings at Risk Register. Aided by a massive grant from the Heritage Lottery Fund and supported by funds raised by local residents, in 2006 Lambeth Council carried out a magnificent restoration, to bring the bandstand back into use.

The bandstand in Edwardian times

The Crystal Palace Band, September 2006

7 – West of the Common

Hollywood and Broadoak

On the short stretch of Nightingale Lane which faces the Common two substantial houses survive. No. 7, once called Hollywood, built in 1782, is notable for its decorations in Coade stone – a popular form of artificial stone developed by Mrs Coade at her Lambeth works in the 1780s and now a lost technique. The doorway with the head in the keystone is a good example. There is also a rare surviving Crown fire insurance plaque over one of the windows.

This house was once the home of the pharmacist and botanist Daniel Bell Hanbury (1794–1882) who had a collection of rare medicinal plants in his garden. It later housed a religious order, and in 2004 opened as Oliver House, an independent Catholic preparatory school.

The next house, Broadoak, was built in 1877 for the widow of Sir Titus Salt, the mill owner who built the town of Saltaire, near Bradford, for his workers. Despite recent research into the family it is not at all clear why Sir Titus Salt came to Clapham. He was elected MP for Bradford in 1859, and appears to have taken a house in Clapham at that time, though he resigned after only two years. He died in 1874, and his widow and two unmarried daughters moved to this Clapham house a few years later.

Adjoining the house is a chapel built in Italian renaissance style in red brick in about 1885. A brightly coloured mosaic over the central window shows the dedication to St Oliver Plunkett, Archbishop of Armagh, who was executed at Tyburn in 1681. It is curious that this chapel appears to have been built while Lady Salt was living at the house, despite the fact that the family were strong Congregationalists. Indeed Dr Guinness Rogers of the Congregational Church in Grafton Square officiated at Lady Salt's funeral in Saltaire in 1893.

The house and chapel are now part of St Francis Xavier Sixth Form College in Malwood Road.

Broadoak, Nightingale Lane

Hightrees House

A substantial nineteenth century villa, called Hightrees, was demolished to make way for this international style block of flats, built in 1938-39. The architect was R W H Jones (1900-1965), who had recently completed Saltdean Lido and hotels, houses and flats at Saltdean (near Brighton) for the Saltdean Estate Co. Curiously, although Jones lived for nearly 30 years after Hightrees was completed, there is no further record of any building by him.

The block is a fine example of the simple lines of the international style, with its horizontal emphasis, concrete balconies, lack of ornament and metal framed windows. A small swimming pool and gymnasium were built in the basement, in recognition of the interest in health and well-being at the time. These have recently been renovated and updated, though sadly the original tiling was lost in an earlier refurbishment. The building has many interesting details, including recessed cupboards outside each flat for deliveries and refuse collection, a combined door-knocker and letterbox on each flat door, which have been retained throughout the building. Some flats are more or less unchanged inside too, and until quite recently some were even occupied by the original tenants.

In the 1970s an additional storey was added on top of the existing block, and this has blended in well. A small formal garden behind, enclosed within the E-shape of the building, gives a peaceful outlook for the internal flats while some on the eastern side of the block, particularly higher up, enjoy spectacular views across the Common.

Hightrees earned a place in legal history in 1946 when Lord Denning (1899-1999), then a junior judge, gave a judgement concerning the payment of ground rent, which was a landmark in the development of laws of property. The building, completed just before the outbreak of the Second World War, was not fully let and an agreement was reached to reduce the rent but no time was specified. Lord Denning's judgement established a new principle of promissory estoppel.

Hightrees House, Nightingale Lane

H M Bateman

On No. 40 Nightingale Lane is a blue plaque recording that the cartoonist H M Bateman lived here. Bateman was born in Australia in 1887 but came to England as a baby. He was a prolific cartoonist whose work appeared in many quality periodicals and in his retirement he painted landscapes of the English countryside. Bateman became well-known in the 1920s and 30s for his series of cartoons, the '*Man Who…,*' which depicted social gaffes. As a result of this series he became the highest paid and most copied cartoonist of his time.

All over London plaques can be found on buildings where famous people have lived. The scheme first started in 1867 by the Royal Society of Arts was taken over by the London County Council, then the Greater London Council and finally, in 1986, by English Heritage. Although the plaques are now blue with white lettering and in a distinctive round format, many of those erected in the early days were chocolate brown. One of these can be seen near Thomas's School in Broomwood Road marking the site of William Wilberforce's house. Other blue plaques in the Clapham area include the following: Gus Elen, music hall comedian, in Thurleigh Avenue; Jack Hobbs, cricketer, in Englewood Road; G A Henty, author, in Lavender Gardens; Edward Thomas, essayist and poet, in Shelgate Road and Natsume Soseki, Japanese novelist, in The Chase.

The blue plaque on H M Bateman's house, No. 40 Nightingale Lane

'The Builder who finished on time'. Cartoon by H M Bateman, around 1930

Broomwood Hall

One of the most remarkable buildings in Nightingale Lane is the massive house in Cambridge cream brick with a Venetian Gothic tower and polished granite columns to the porch and bay windows, which is now the home of Broomwood Hall school. The house, built in 1874, was originally called Fairseat. The architect Rowland Plumbe was also responsible for an extension to Springfield Hospital nearby, the rebuilding of the London Hospital, several churches as well as houses. Like many of the large houses in the area in due course the house was too large for a family home, and by the 1940s it had become one of the many trade union headquarters in Clapham, that of the National Union of Printing, Book–Binding and Paper Workers.

After further changes of use the building was bought by the expanding local Broomwood Hall school in 1988 and now houses their Upper school. The building has been considerably enlarged at various times, including the addition of a completely new storey in 1971.

On the boundary wall of the property are the remains of a folly structure, as well as brick piers and railings. These might be the remains of a building in the grounds of a large house belonging to William Lynn which once stood where Nightingale Square now is. There is a detailed description of a hermitage at the edge of his grounds, which was *'built as a Toy by Mr Lynn and furnished with the most scrupulous exactness and very good taste, both outside and in… and possesses every convenience for a Hermit who wants but little here below'*. The hermitage did, in fact, have a library with some illuminated missals on vellum, walls painted with Gothic designs, windows with pictures in the stained glass and *'plenty of live Ducks in the Pond in front and probably Eels in the ditch behind'*.

Headquarters of the National Union of Printing, Book-Binding and Paper Workers, No. 74 Nightingale Lane, around 1965

Thomas Collcutt and George Jennings

The ornate group of houses at Nos. 69-79 Nightingale Lane were built in 1879 by Thomas Collcutt and George Jennings, possibly for the directors of the Royal Doulton factory which was in Lambeth. The houses are in red brick with details in terracotta or faience, which was very fashionable at the time. By the 1870s the Doulton factory, founded in the 1820s, was one of the leading manufacturers.

The keystones to the ground floor windows are embossed with a circular inscription *'Jennings Poole Dorset'*. For some time the connection between Lambeth and Poole was not known, but recent research has revealed that the material for these was prepared at the works of George Jennings in Poole.

After working for a lead and glass merchant and then for a plumber, George Jennings left his native village, Parkstone, near Poole to seek his fortune in London. He eventually established a successful sanitary ware business, mainly as a result of his invention of *'indiarubber tube taps'*. He became a leading expert on sanitary ware and was responsible for the sanitary arrangements at the Great Exhibition in Hyde Park in 1851 and again when the Crystal Palace was moved to Sydenham. At one time it was said that there was scarcely a house of importance or a hotel in London in which his appliances were not used.

Jennings was also an expert on heating and ventilation. He leased extensive clay beds at Parkstone where he built kilns and pottery works for the manufacture of his stoneware pipes and terracotta and faience decorations. He later moved into property development in close association with Collcutt. In Clapham they built some houses in Ferndale Road as well as in Nightingale Lane. In 1879 Jennings himself moved to No. 79 from Ferndale (now Nightingale House), the large house further along Nightingale Lane which he had built some years earlier. However, his glittering career came to an untimely end in 1882 when he was thrown from a gig near Albert Bridge. Although his injuries were not thought at the time to be life threatening, he died some weeks later in his Nightingale Lane house.

Window showing faience decorations by George Jennings, No. 71 Nightingale Lane

St Luke's Church

The first church on this site was a temporary iron structure erected in 1874 on a corner of the grounds of the former Old Park House. In that year Canon John Erskine-Clarke, the founder and first vicar of St Luke's, purchased the part of the grounds where the lake and ice-house of Old Park House had once been. He described the site where *'there was a pond, famous for water lilies, and a mound nearly as high as the present houses, with three or four well grown scotch firs on the top'.* The mound was removed when Old Park Avenue was built.

The iron church was formerly in Battersea Rise, where it had been used by the parishioners while their new church, St Mark's, was being built. It was not until 1882 that a committee was formed to promote the building of a brick church for St Luke's. The Bishop of Rochester wrote *'A fine red-brick Basilica is the one thing of all others I wish to see. Who will build us one?'*

The answer was provided by the architect F W Hunt and builders J Johnson & Co. of Wandsworth. In 1883 the chancel and south transept were dedicated by the Bishop and a notice announced: *'This portion of the Church will contain 288 chairs – so that with the Iron Church annexed there will be room for about 600 worshippers with ample choir arrangements'.* The iron church was removed in 1888 when the new church was complete except for the tower and the baptistery. The tall north-west tower with its open bell chamber and pyramid shaped copper roof was completed in 1892 and the baptistery

St Luke's Church, Ramsden Road

was added seven years later. At the time the church was still a *'chapel of ease'* for St Mary's Battersea, and did not become an independent parish church until 1901.

The original main entrance to the church was through a porch formed by the ground floor of the tower. The large stone at the head of this arch is carved and enriched with marble and coloured spar bosses. The church is in the style of a red brick Italian basilica, and many of the fittings are in Italian style. Amongst these are an alabaster font supported on Verona marble columns, mosaics of the four evangelists, an alabaster lectern in the shape of an angel and an alabaster chancel screen with coloured marble pillars – red from Verona, yellow from Siena, pale red from Turkey and green from Greece. The font – a gift of local children – has a large cover, which is raised by a most ingenious counterweight system. St Luke's is said to be the first church in London to be lit by electricity, which was installed in 1903 as the gift of a parishioner. The original bronze electric light switches framed in marble survive (no longer in use), as do the electroliers in the nave, which were designed from a pendant jewel by Benvenuto Cellini in the Pitti Palace in Florence.

In 2003 a new Community Hall was built, adjoining and linked to the church, by local architect Stephen Buck.

Interior of St Luke's Church

Thomas's School

Erected close to the site of Broomwood House, the home of William Wilberforce during his campaign against slavery, this impressive building is one of the most striking of the schools designed for the London County Council by the T J Bailey, architect of the Schools Board for London. The twin circular staircase towers can be seen from a considerable distance. The school was completed in 1907 and Clapham County Secondary School for Girls moved there from the premises on North Side which it had long outgrown.

The school was remarkable at the time for being well equipped with a spacious hall, science laboratories and a gymnasium. In the 1930s, to celebrate the school's twenty-first birthday, a library was built at a cost of £500, the gift of former students. Clapham County Secondary School enjoyed a high reputation and had several distinguished pupils, including the novelist Pamela Hansford Johnson, whoset several of her novels in Clapham. Her autobiography gives a fascinating description of life in Clapham in the 1930s and of her romance with the poet Dylan Thomas, who stayed at her home in Battersea Rise.

Following educational reforms the school was renamed Walsingham in 1976 and after another reorganisation it became redundant in the late 1980s. After a period of uncertainty the freehold of the building was purchased by Thomas's London Day Schools in 1992 and the following year it opened as an independent coeducational preparatory school, known as Thomas's Clapham. There has been new building and refurbishment over the years, but the original buildings still provide excellent facilities for the school.

Thomas's School, Broomwood Road

William Wilberforce. Watercolour by George Richmond, 1833

Houses on West Side

Of the large houses with extensive gardens which once lined the west side of Clapham Common, only a very few survive. The only one at the southern end is No. 21, Heathfield, a fine detached brick house with a semi-circular porch built in 1806 probably by James Burton, father of the architect Decimus Burton. Once the home of Edward Colman of the mustard family, the house was later a hostel for the elderly before being refurbished as a single family residence in the 1990s. The large garden had long since disappeared for the building of the streets behind.

At the northern end of West Side a group of late eighteenth century houses remain. Nos. 81 and 82 are a pair, which have both now been restored to family use after years of institutional use and neglect. In 2004 a modern house, skilfully designed round an atrium, was built on part of the garden behind No. 81 replacing a garage dealing in classic cars. The original pair of coach houses between Nos. 82 and 83 survive and have been restored.

The group is completed by two detached houses of similar date, and No. 85 which dates from the mid-nineteenth century. All are substantial houses and reminders of how the borders of the Common would once have looked. Those who have lived in these houses include the opera singer Adelina Patti, Sir William Augustus Fraser MP and friend of Disraeli, and Adam Worth, alias Henry Raymond, who lived here as a respectable Victorian gentleman while following a career as an international bank robber and forger.

Where the former mansions were demolished, mostly around the turn of the twentieth century, attractive terraces of houses line the road. Most of these retain many original features including canopied porches with balconettes over, stained glass in panelled doors and moulded brick decorations.

Clapham Common West Side, with elms felled after Dutch Elm Disease, 1975

Battersea Rise House

In 1792 Henry Thornton bought Battersea Rise (as it was originally called, 'House' was added later), just off the west side of the Common, which was to become the centre of the activities of the Clapham Sect. William Wilberforce lived here with Henry Thornton until they both married in 1797 when Thornton built another house, Broomfield, on his estate into which Wilberforce moved.

Battersea Rise was *'a large and commodious mansion of no particular architectural merit, but designed for comfort'*. The beautiful grounds were described by several visitors including, the American ornithologist, J J Audubon, who wrote: *'I walked through avenues of foreign trees and shrubs, amongst which were tulip-trees, larches, and cypresses from America. Many birds were here, some searching for food, while others gave vent to their happy feelings in harmonious concerts. The house itself was covered with vines, the front a mass of blooming roses exuberant with perfume. What a delightful feast I had in this peaceful spot!'*

The house had a library, *'oval in shape and curiously wainscoted on every side with books, except where it opened on to the lawn'* which is said to have been designed by William Pitt the Younger, a friend of Thornton's and frequent visitor to the house.

Henry Thornton's son, another Henry, inherited the house in 1815 when he was only 15 years old, and lived there with his sisters. In 1833 his new wife Harriet Dealtry moved in. On her death some years later he caused a sensation by announcing that he wished to marry her sister, Emily. Such a marriage was not then allowed in England so the ceremony took place abroad, and Henry's sister, Marianne, showed her disapproval by moving out to a house on the other side of the Common. Marianne's great-nephew was the author, E M Forster, who wrote a biography of her based on the volumes of recollections she compiled.

Henry Thornton's widow continued to live at Battersea Rise House after his death with her daughter and son-in-law,

Percy Thornton MP. However, Henry Thornton's will explicitly directed that his estate be sold and the proceeds should be divided between his descendants on his widow's death.

The property therefore was sold in 1907 for £51,000.

Battersea Rise House, around 1904. Drawing by E E Briscoe

Battersea Rise House was the last of the the great houses on West Side to be demolished for development. Over the preceding decades the grounds around these houses stretching back almost to Northcote Road had been a magnet for developers. Between about 1880 and 1920 the grid of streets between Clapham and Wandsworth Commons was developed. Most houses were built in short terraces, and within each street one can often detect the different builders who were active.

While the earlier houses are similar to the Victorian terraces all around the Common, those built between about 1910 and the early 1920s show many interesting Art Nouveau details. Alfriston Road, one of several streets developed on the grounds of Battersea Rise House by Edwin Evans from 1910, is particularly attractive. Many houses have the distinctive clay tile roofs, fretwork timber porches, stained glass and tiling reminiscent of the work of Voysey, who did in fact design a few houses for clients in South London. The outstanding house in the street, The Cottage (No. 90) built by W H George in 1914, survives totally unspoilt with its roughcast render over red brick, painted wooden shutters and '1914' set over the door in clay tiles.

No. 90 Alfriston Road

Index

If you would like to find out more about Clapham you may be interested in these Clapham Society publications

Publications
may be obtained
from:
Alyson Wilson
22 Crescent Grove
London SW4 7AH

Telephone: 020 7622 6360

Email: alysonwilson.sw4@virgin.net

Personal callers by prior arrangement

Postage and packing £2 per book
50p for up to 3 walks

Cheques payable to:
The Clapham Society

The Clapham Sect

MARGARET BRYANT
(April 2004) 64 pages.
The story of a group of people whose activities changed the world. Wealthy Clapham businessmen and religious philanthropists, they fought to change the moral climate of their times, and campaigned against the injustices of slavery and the slave trade. Led by William Wilberforce in Parliament, their greatest achievement was the outlawing of the Atlantic slave trade in 1807. Margaret Bryant paints a vivid picture of these remarkable people and their lives in late eighteenth century Clapham and reminds us how much our modern world owes to them.
£6.00 (members)
or £7.50 (non-members)

Clapham in the Twentieth Century

(2002) 232 pages.
A collection of letters, diaries and memories of Clapham during the century, from Graham Greene, Jack Hobbs and Noel Coward to immigrants from the West Indies, Poland and Kosovo, local businessmen, shopkeepers and school-children. In the words of those who witnessed them, the book tracks the changes in Clapham from the last years of Queen Victoria's reign through two World Wars, depression, revival and gentrification to the lively, popular family area that it had become by 2000.
£10.00 (members)
or £11.95 (non-members)

The Buildings of Clapham

(2000) 236 pages.
A history of the development of Clapham and its buildings with street-by-street gazetteer giving date, builder, architect, noteworthy features of each building and information on interesting former residents. Illustrated with maps – old and new – archive photographs and drawings of architectural details. Detailed glossary and index.
£10.00 (members)
or £11.95 (non-members)

Self-guided walks leaflets

Each covering a different
area of Clapham.
Price 50p each.

Available now:
1 Old Clapham
2 Clapham North
3 Around Nightingale Lane
4 Clapham Common
5 South Side
6 West Side

In preparation:
Around Park Hill
North Side
Clapham High Street

Join the Clapham Society.....

.....if you are interested in Clapham,

its community, its businesses, its amenities
and its buildings and are concerned to
protect and enhance its character

Membership is £6 per year for an individual
or £9 for a family

For a membership application form contact:

The Membership Secretary
Jennifer Everett
30 Trinity Close
London SW4 0JD

Telephone: 020 7627 4770

Our aims

We aim to improve
the quality of life in Clapham
and strengthen its identity
and sense of community

We seek to promote
excellence in new
developments as well
as conservation of the
best features of the past

We want Clapham
to be a vibrant, exciting
and safe place to live,
with job opportunities
and good shopping and
leisure amenities

Our activities

We fight to protect the special character of
Clapham, its conservation areas and buildings
of historic and architectural interest

We are consulted on current planning
and development proposals and, if necessary,
we present evidence to formal planning enquiries

We run a programme of events including
talks on local and wider London topics,
and walks around Clapham which focus on
new developments as well as local history

We produce and distribute to members and
key local people a monthly newsletter giving
information and opinions on current and
impending issues and events

We foster and maintain constructive relationships
with local councillors and officers in order to
present effectively the views of the Society
and its members

We liaise and consult with other amenity groups

We publish books about the area and its history,
guided walk leaflets and cards

We organise parties and social gatherings for
members and their guests in houses
and gardens of interest

We run a local history group

The Clapham Society
www.outlines.org.uk/claphamsociety/

Discovering Clapham

The Clapham Society

2007